THINK ON THIS

DAILY WISDOM TO NAVIGATE
A MISGUIDED WORLD

BRENT RUDOSKI

Think on This

Printed in Canada.

Editing by Val Keen, Jean Ramage, and Katie Giles
Cover design by Tosin Akinpelu
Artwork by Arden Fehr

ISBN: 978-1-988316-32-1

Faith Alive Press
Telephone: 306-652-2230

Mailing address:
Site 600 Comp 211 RR6
Saskatoon SK S7K 3J9
www.fafc.ca info@fafc.ca

Cataloguing in publication may be obtained through Library and Archives Canada.

Contents

WEEK 1– WISDOM

Day 1

Wisdom is the principal thing; Therefore, get wisdom.
And in all your getting, get understanding.
Proverbs 4:7

King Solomon, the man credited with penning the book of Proverbs, was considered the wisest who ever lived. When Solomon was appointed King of Israel, God came to him and asked him one question, *"Ask! What shall I give you?"* Wait a minute! What? Anything? Are you kidding me? Wow! What would your answer be? Probably something like this, *"Uh, I'll take a million dollars, no wait, ten million dollars, a long, healthy life, popularity aaaand, I think, fame. Yes, I want to be famous and powerful. Oh, I want to live in a mansion and have servants, too. Oh, one more thing, I don't want to work. Is that too much, Lord?"*

However, Solomon didn't ask for anything like that; instead, he asked for the wisdom to wisely rule his people. In 2 Chronicles 11-12, God replied, *"Because you didn't ask for wealth, or honour, or the lives of your enemies and long life, I will give you the wisdom you asked for and all these things you didn't, and in such a manner as has never been seen with the kings before you or will be after you."*

As a result of gaining Godly wisdom, Solomon was able to accomplish many things, and through wisdom, he achieved great success and wealth. His wisdom became a worldwide phenomenon, so much so that even the great Queen of Sheba came to hear him. After asking Solomon many hard questions, and hearing his wisdom, she was astounded, and blessed him with an abundance of treasures.

King Solomon surpassed all the kings of the earth in riches and wisdom. He was held in such high regard that every king on earth sought time in his presence to hear this extraordinary wisdom God had put in his heart.

"Wisdom is the right use of knowledge."

Charles Spurgeon

There are many things that we can acquire in life. We can spend our lives obtaining everything, but only wisdom will truly help us in life.

Wisdom is the main thing that Solomon promoted, and no wonder, it gave him everything. I pray today that Solomon's prayer would become your prayer.

THINK ON THIS... Are you working harder or smarter? When you take the time to sharpen your axe with wisdom, success will soon follow.

WEEK 1
WISDOM

Day 2

The fear of the Lord is the beginning of wisdom, and the knowledge of the Holy One is understanding.

Proverbs 9:10

How do we begin to acquire wisdom? How does one become wise? Is there a formula for this?

Perhaps if we wait until we are older, wisdom will come to us, but that is not guaranteed. Age doesn't necessarily provide wisdom. As the old saying goes, *"There is no fool like an old fool."* What is the meaning of this statement? The answer is that mature people are expected to know better, but often they do outrageously foolish things, especially regarding romantic liaisons. It's sometimes painful to watch the elderly do unwise things.

Proverbs 13:20 tells us that, *"He who walks with the wise will be wise, but the companion of fools will be destroyed."*

You don't have to be older to exhibit wisdom. It can begin at any age by merely having great respect and honour for the Lord. After all, He created everything, including you, by His infinite wisdom and power. If we hang around the One who is Wisdom, how can we not obtain wisdom? The same is true in everyday life. We become like those with whom we hang around. If I want wisdom concerning a certain thing, I must get it from those people who have it. For instance, if I want to gain a better grip on my finances, I would not look to the poor or homeless for advice. I would talk to people who are financially stable and successful. Their wisdom can become mine.

"A wise owl sat on an oak, the more he saw the less he spoke, the less he spoke the more he heard. Why aren't we like the wise old bird?"

Charles M. Schulz

Anyone who desires to be wise need only begin to fear the Lord by receiving God's instruction, guidance, and becoming a doer of His Word. How do we gain wisdom? Listen to God and listen to wise people. If you do that, wisdom will surely be yours.

THINK ON THIS...

You will become like the people you hang with. Choose your friends wisely.

WEEK 1
WISDOM

Day 3

Happy is the man who finds wisdom, and the man who gains understanding; For her proceeds are better than the profits of silver, and her gain than fine gold. She is more precious than rubies, and all the things you may desire cannot compare with her.

Proverbs 3:13-15

The *Merriam-Webster Collegiate Thesaurus* describes wisdom as:

1. Knowledge, good sense, and good judgment
2. A wise attitude, belief, or course of action

I think we can all agree that if a person has wisdom, their life has the potential to be better. Wise men see what's ahead and make the necessary plans. Wise people see evil and walk around it. They consider their path and walk accordingly. Wise people listen to instruction and use it to benefit their lives.

If you use wisdom in life, you will be happy, and who doesn't want that? Wisdom produces happiness because, by it, a person will make good and proper decisions and escape the pitfalls of life.

"Wisdom is the reward you get for a lifetime of listening when you'd have preferred to talk."

Doug Larson

We could say that wisdom is the ability to use knowledge, or good sense, to gain understanding in all aspects of life. So precious was it that Solomon declared it's far better to acquire wisdom than money. He would know, being he was the richest man of his time. Yes, money can make life better, and we do need it, but without wisdom, so many have squandered it. And that, my friends, would certainly lead to unhappiness, wouldn't it? Statistics prove that one out of every three lottery winners end up bankrupt. Money is a tool like any other, and it takes wisdom to use it wisely. So please, do yourself a favour - seek wisdom, and do whatever it takes to acquire it. The happiness you save may be your own!

THINK ON THIS...

Wisdom can be found if you look hard enough to find it.

WEEK 1
WISDOM

Day 4

My son, eat honey because it is good, and the honeycomb which is sweet to your taste; So shall the knowledge of wisdom be to your soul; If you have found it, there is a prospect, and your hope will not be cut off.

Proverbs 24:13-14

Have you ever done something that left a bad taste in your mouth, and the nasty result was that the hope for your future diminished? Too many bad choices will definitely ruin the flavour of life. What you thought would be sweet has turned sour and bitter. That is hard to bear. The hope that was once strong and vibrant is now almost gone, and despair is trying to creep in. What can you do about it? Know this first - you are not alone. God has given us His Word to guide and direct us. Too often, we make wrong choices or decisions because we don't consult God's Word or ask a wise person to show us the way.

Yes, maybe you've made some dumb moves, but you aren't stuck there forever. I have paid dearly for the lack of wisdom, but the more I learned of God and His ways, the better my life became. So, read and study the Word of God, and learn to love its taste as you would honey. The knowledge and wisdom you will gain in your soul will produce hope and a better future for you. It won't take long and that bitter taste in your mouth will become sweet.

"Indecision is a decision."

Anonymous

THINK ON THIS...

Don't make any decisions until you have consulted the Word of God.

WEEK 1
WISDOM

Day 5

> If the ax is dull, and one does not sharpen the edge, then he must use more strength; but wisdom brings success.
>
> Ecclesiastes 10:10

Work smarter, not harder, is the old adage, and sometimes it's true. While there are times when we must roll up our sleeves and put in an old-fashioned day of work, wisdom can save us time and energy. Of course, there are stints when working extra hard doesn't seem like it's enough, or we work and work, and work, but nothing changes. Maybe on those days, it would be wiser to sit back and ponder. Yes, I said ponder. This means to take time to consider and weigh what we are doing and try to find a better, more efficient manner to get it done. Taking time to ponder on something is not a waste. It will end up saving you time and even money in the long run.

> *"We learn wisdom from failure much more than from success. We often discover what will do, by finding out what will not do; and probably he who never made a mistake never made a discovery."*
>
> Samuel Smiles

I know there are several different ways to accomplish our goals in life. The question is, which one employs the wisdom of God to achieve the goal in a superior manner?

If you have ever used an axe to chop wood, you know full well how much harder it is to cut when its edge is dull. A sharp blade cuts quicker and cleaner and is more efficient. Yes, it will still cut when dull, but will require more energy. Which axe would you prefer to use - dull or sharp? Wisdom is the sharp ax, so seek to be wise in all your affairs.

THINK ON THIS... Are you working harder or smarter? When you take the time to sharpen your axe with wisdom, success will soon follow.

WEEK 2 – FOOLISHNESS

Day 6

The fear of the Lord is the beginning of knowledge,
but fools despise wisdom and instruction.

Proverbs 1:7

Man's quest for knowledge is never-ending. The increase of knowledge is undoubtedly beneficial, but earthly or natural insight will only help us to a point. Real understanding begins as we come to know the Holy One, and this divine information produces what is referred to as *"the fear of the Lord."*

> *"Fear of God is a liberating emotion, freeing one from a disabling fear of evil, powerful people. This needs to be emphasized because many people see fear of God as onerous rather than liberating."*
>
> Dennis Prager,
> *The Rational Bible: Exodus*

Knowledge is essential in life if we want to learn, grow, and understand things, but having a healthy respect for the knowledge of God adds a unique and powerful dimension to our lives. Because knowledge is so valuable, many have turned to wrong sources in their pursuit of it. People look to the stars, the spirits, the occult, and the ancient, trying to discover what they believe are the secrets to life, but the true source of life is found only in the Lord. He is the One who created the heavens and the earth and is the ultimate source of all knowledge. The moment you recognize that God is God and that He is the creator of all things, true knowledge starts to flow. Psalm 14:1 says, *"The fool has said in his heart, "there is no God;""* however, you only need to take a good, long look around and His handiwork is clearly visible. The heavens declare His majesty and the stars shout all night long of His great knowledge and power.

THINK ON THIS... Are you open to receive instructions from the wise and knowledgeable?

WEEK 2
FOOLISHNESS

Day 7

For the turning away of the simple will slay them,
and the complacency of fools will destroy them.

Proverbs 1:32

Who wants to be called a fool? I sure don't, yet that's precisely what the writer calls people who fail to take seriously what really matters in life. Hearing and receiving Godly instruction, avoiding all evil, and having a heart for the Lord, are life-producing, and anyone complacent about them will pay the price. It's foolish to wander away from the Lord and suppose that it doesn't matter. Believe me, it does.

> *"The tragedy of life is not found in failure, but in complacency. Not in you doing too much but doing too little. Not in you living above your means, but below your capacity. It's not failure but aiming too low, that is life's great tragedy."*
>
> Benjamin E. Mays

When I was twelve years old, I was lying in bed one night and praying to God. As I talked, it was like my words went up to the ceiling and bounced right back at me. After that, I just didn't care anymore. I felt slighted by God and gave up all restraint and went wild. I partied, did drugs, drank alcohol constantly, and basically lived an extremely foolish life.

Fast forward ten years, and I had become a mess. My body was worn out, my mind was out of whack, I was deeply in debt, and bound up by evil forces. Having foolishly stopped doing what was right, I was now paying the price for it. Believing myself to be wise, I had become a fool. Thank God for His great mercy and grace as He found me and saved me. While I would never consider myself extremely wise, I did become a whole lot smarter. I found out that by having a fear of God, listening to His Word and His people, my life began to change for the better. Now, many years later, I can truly testify of the power of following the Lord.

THINK ON THIS...

Would others call you wise or foolish?

WEEK 2
FOOLISHNESS

Day 8

The wise watch their steps and avoid evil;
fools are headstrong and reckless.
Proverbs 14:16 Message

The old idiom, *"Fools rush in where angels fear to tread,"* is rightly said, for a reckless attitude can lead to ruin. Headstrong - have you ever met anyone who fits this description? I've met some and have been that way myself. Sometimes we can be so stubborn, even when wrong, just so we can say, *"I do what I want, and nobody tells me any different."* It's the School of Hard Knocks for those who refuse to listen to counsel or correction. Wise people take their time to ponder the next step and won't be coerced into moving faster than they should.

"Take time for deliberation. Haste spoils everything."
Statius

Some folks are easily fooled by the glitter of a good deal or the opportunity to make a fast buck. They rush in headstrong and reckless, blinded by desire, and unwilling to see the danger. Recklessness is one sure-fire way to bring trouble into our lives. It's one thing to move quickly, when necessary, but to be hasty is to be bereft of the wisdom to see the difference. People who cast off caution will eventually bear the consequences of it. Stephen Colbert said, *"Never throw caution to the wind; it could whip back into your eyes and blind you."* In other words, watch your steps, for the next one could be dangerous. Before you jump, make sure you can actually make it. Some people take too long to make decisions or move because of fear, but I'm talking about using wisdom to make the best choice. If what's offered to you seems too good to be true, then it probably is.

THINK ON THIS... Don't be like the horse that strains to run ahead or the donkey that refuses to budge and lags behind. Somewhere in the middle is the gait of success.

WEEK 2
Foolishness

Day 9

There's only one kind of person who is worse than a fool:
the impetuous one who speaks without thinking first.

Proverbs 29:20 TPT

Have you ever been labelled a fool or worse than a fool? Is there anything more horrible than that? I don't want to be called a fool, let alone worse than one. Speaking before you think is extremely foolish. I can attest to this, having made this mistake many times. If you are a leader who speaks into people's lives, it's easy to do. Another Proverb speaks of the shame and folly of those who answer before they hear the whole matter. It's tempting to hear only a part of the situation and think we know the answer. It seems the older I get, the worse this has become because I sometimes lack patience. It would be like walking into a room, only hearing part of the conversation, and then offering our opinion or advice. Usually, this results in everyone looking at you with that mostly polite yet true, *"What an idiot!"* facial expression. Every time this happens, I inwardly kick myself for being a fool, and yet it seems to happen time and time again. I'm learning to take the time to really listen, and I must admit to finding it quite challenging, typically because I'm very impatient. I guess this is why God gave us two ears and only one mouth.

"Speak when you are angry, and you will make the best speech you will ever regret."

Ambrose Bierce

James, the half-brother of Jesus, had this to say in chapter one, verse nineteen, *"Let every man be swift to hear and slow to speak."* Unfortunately, most people are too quick to speak and very slow to hear. I think we are in love with the sound of our own voices. If the people around you are saying, *"Would you please just listen?"* perhaps less lip movement is needed. He who has ears to hear, let him listen.

THINK ON THIS...

Before you speak, take the time to think about it.

Week 2
Foolishness

Day 10

Only a fool despises a parent's discipline;
whoever learns from correction is wise.
Proverbs 15:5 NLT

I'm always amazed at how people dislike being corrected. It must be because they feel like they are being rejected or put down. However, the opposite is true, for when one is corrected, it's because they are loved. Correction is for the sole purpose of learning. If we never receive instruction, we cannot learn from our mistakes. Unfortunately, there is something in most of us that hates to be challenged. We have an almost unconscious desire to be right.

In the early nineties, I was working in a hotel. After being there for six months, my employee evaluation came up. The guy who was over me called me into his office and laid it out. My evaluation was excellent, except for one thing. I listened as he told me what it was, but inside I rejected it. While driving home that evening, I rehearsed the matter in my head and became very upset. Who does he think he is to tell me, a King's kid, with God's grace on me, born again, righteous in God's sight, and an all-around great guy, that I had something to correct? Humph, not a chance. At that very second, I heard the Holy Ghost speak to me in a clear voice saying, *"He's right, you know, you should listen to him."* What? Really? You've got to be kidding me. It's funny because for some strange reason I believed I was exempt from earthly or natural human correction. After all, I had God in me, and if I were to be corrected, it would, of course, come from Him.

Boy was I ever wrong! When I re-evaluated what he said about me, I realized it was the truth, and right then and there, I determined I would change. This happened early in my Christian walk, and I learned that God sometimes uses people to correct and help us get better. Such a valuable lesson! The question for all of us is will we allow people to do it?

> *"Let me never fall into the vulgar mistake of dreaming that I am persecuted whenever I am contradicted."*
>
> Ralph Waldo Emerson,
> *Emerson in His Journals*

Since then, I've listened to anyone who has tried to correct me or offer their advice or tell me something contrary. How often has someone come to me after I have preached and challenged or completely differed with me on a point? Instead of quickly rejecting their words, I now take a little time to reflect and evaluate. I like to ask myself, *"Is there some truth in there? Can I learn from it?"* The next time your opinion is challenged, or you are corrected, don't get upset; take it, and see if there is any wisdom there for you. I guarantee you will benefit greatly from it.

THINK ON THIS... How do you feel when you are corrected or challenged in some way?

WEEK 3 – INTEGRITY

Day 11

...for receiving wise instruction in righteousness,
justice, and integrity.

Proverbs 1:3 HCSB

The book of Proverbs has a lot to say about integrity, a trait that easily eludes us. Integrity is doing what's right when we feel pressured to do wrong. Having integrity means doing the right thing in tough or difficult times. It's a personality trait that we admire since it means a person has a moral compass that doesn't waver. It means having "wholeness" of character, just as an *integer* is a "whole number" with no fractions. There is no deviation in its nature. You either have it, or you don't. The decisions you make in life reveal your level of integrity.

Physical objects can display integrity too — if you're going over a rickety old bridge that sways in the wind, you might question its structural integrity. Just as you cannot trust a broken-down bridge, neither should you trust a person who lacks integrity.

Integrity is also one of God's greatest attributes. Because of His great integrity, God is always trustworthy. If HE said it, He will do it. He is not a man that lies or gives in when it's convenient to do so. His yes is yes and amen. God is not wishy-washy; He is the one who is consistent and constant in our lives. I love the fact that God never changes, and HE is the same yesterday, today, and forever. What He promises, HE will fulfill.

In our lives, people will let us down; they will promise something and never deliver. You will feel betrayed and start to lose trust in them, but always remember, God can be trusted. He will never let you down. We will eventually let Him down, but He cannot let us down. He is faithful even when we are not. He is true to His own Word. That, my friends, is called integrity!

> *"Your word is your honour. If you say you are going to do something, then you need to do it."*
>
> Joyce Meyer

Back when I was a teenager, a guy who I thought was a good friend decided to do something different than what we had initially planned. I guess he got a better offer. Of course, I was disappointed. I realized that some folks lacked the character trait of integrity. They promise one thing, but later, renege on it. That incident caused me to look at myself, first at my immaturity, for being hurt over it, and secondly, it produced a desire in me to always keep my promises. Since that incident, I have tried to keep my word to people, even if it is inconvenient or uncomfortable. Walking in integrity isn't always easy, but it is crucial, and brings incredible blessings.

THINK ON THIS...

The next time you feel pressured to change your mind after you've given your word, don't give in. Keep your word. You will become a better person for it. God blesses those who walk in integrity, for they are emulating Him.

WEEK 3
INTEGRITY

Day 12

His wife said to him, "Do you still retain your integrity? Curse God and die!"

Job 2:9 HCSB

The saying, *"Never judge a man until you've walked a mile in his shoes,"* is well known. I cannot possibly imagine the pain and hurt Job experienced when his life was turned upside down by Satan's persecutions and hatred. Why did Satan dislike Job? Because God had raved to him about Job, and particularly, his outstanding integrity. Job was a man who hated evil, loved God, and had faith that He was good. God had tremendously blessed Job and covered him with protection and favour. Satan's response to this was, *"Of course he keeps his integrity. You have sheltered him, but take all that away, and his great character will quickly go out the window."* So, God allowed Job to experience the worst of suffering; more than most people will ever see in life. Everything he had was affected in some manner - family, livestock, even his health, and yet, he would not blame God. Job's wife, having given in to despair, encouraged him to do the same, but he wouldn't. Why? One word - integrity!

"The one who lives with integrity will be helped, but one who distorts right and wrong will suddenly fall."

Proverbs 28:18 HCSB

"Winning is nice if we don't lose our integrity in the process."

Harold Henbak

When life is a struggle and times get tough, it's easy to begin losing faith in God's goodness. The enemy of our souls has taken on the mandate to do his very best to cause us to question and eventually give up our faith. One thing I'm convinced of is that our faith will be tested, but if we stay strong in integrity, we will come out as gold tried in the fire, something that pleases God. When we keep our faith in difficult circumstances, it's called integrity. The enemy wants to cause confusion and frustration, distort our view of God, and ultimately cause us to lose our love for Him. But we, like Job, fully understand that God is good and has no darkness at all. He is light, and that light will push out any darkness that tries to overcome us. Trust in God, especially when life goes sour. When life hands you a lemon, what should you do? Make lemonade, of course. As we keep our integrity when it comes to God's goodness, He will turn life's bitter areas into sweet. HE is our ever-present help in times of trouble. And we know the outcome of Job's life, don't we? He was extremely blessed. Integrity pays off!

THINK ON THIS... Don't give in to the pressure to blame God when life throws you a curve. Instead, be like Job and choose to trust God. Your integrity will produce an excellent harvest of God's goodness in your life.

WEEK 3
INTEGRITY

Day 13

Better a poor man who lives with integrity than someone who has deceitful lips and is a fool.

Proverbs 19:1 HCSB

If you had your "druthers," would you rather be rich or poor? I'm going to go out on a limb here and say, rich. No one wants to be poor. But if you find yourself in this situation, there is a "better" attached to it. It's better to be poor and have integrity than be rich and have none. This Proverb doesn't mention rich, but it infers it. You'll find many Proverbs that contrast the rich and poor. Rich isn't always good, and poor isn't necessarily bad; what matters is who you are. One would think that being rich is the best thing no matter what a person is like, but God says no. In His sight, one who is financially poor, but rich in integrity holds a superior position. If a person is wealthy but lacks integrity, he is classified as a fool.

> *"If you don't have integrity, you have nothing. You can't buy it. You can have all the money in the world, but if you are not a moral and ethical person, you really have nothing."*
>
> Henry Kravis

Is it great to have money? Yes. Can money buy you everything you want? Yes, but only to a point; it can't purchase good godly character. Money can't help a person keep his word, do what's right in tough times, or stand firm when tempted to do otherwise. Money can't buy love, nor can it bring true happiness.

All the money in the whole world won't benefit a person if they have little or no integrity. Integrity is one of the few things money cannot buy. So, whether you are rich or poor, integrity matters. However, it is doubly great if a person has both wealth and integrity - then they are truly rich!

THINK ON THIS...

Does the love of money tempt you to lose your integrity? For instance, it's so much easier to give God a percentage of $100 than $10,000. If you have integrity, the amount won't matter.

WEEK 3
INTEGRITY

Day 14

Surely You desire integrity in the inner self,
and You teach me wisdom deep within.

Psalm 51:6 HCSB

Who are you? Really? I don't mean the person you see when you look in a mirror, but the one on the inside that only God sees. That is the real you. Jesus once said, *"Out of the abundance of the heart the mouth speaks,"* meaning that your mouth will ultimately disclose what actually goes on in your inner self. The person you are on the inside will eventually make its way to the outside. It can't be stopped. God desires us to be people of integrity, and it must come from a genuine heart.

> *"If you have to hide from someone what you're doing, then you know in your heart what you are doing is wrong."*
>
> AddictsToday.com

The problem with integrity is it's usually needed most in times of extreme pressure or dire circumstances. Like a faulty pipe, leaks will show up when the pressure is on. Do you remember when Potiphar's beautiful wife tried to seduce Joseph? She tried for months on end but to no avail. Eventually, she grew bold enough to demand that he lay with her. Joseph's integrity kicked in, and he fled the scene, saying to himself, *"How can I do this thing and sin against God?"* If Joseph had not believed in integrity or didn't have it on the inside, he might have given in to the temptation. When things happen suddenly, we don't have the luxury of looking inside the tickle trunk for an hour to find what we need to handle the situation. Either it's there, or it's not. It's vitally important that we have integrity inside us so that when unexpected temptations arise, we will stay true to God and ourselves. You are in integrity when your life on the outside matches who you are on the inside.

THINK ON THIS... Do you value integrity, or do you give it up depending on the circumstances you're facing?

WEEK 3
INTEGRITY

Day 15

The integrity of the upright guides them, but the perversity of the treacherous destroys them.

Proverbs 11:3 HCSB

When you are a person of integrity, you're never in a dither about what you should do. Integrity is a guide for life because it takes away all the other options. Situational ethics should not enter the equation of the decision-making process. You already know what you are going to do beforehand. Here's an example that our family has followed for most of our Christian lives. When it's time to go to church, we go to church. We have a pre-set on the church dial of our lives that leaves no room for anything else. We made a quality decision to go to bed on Saturday nights at a decent time, thus eliminating sleeping in on Sunday mornings. As a result, we also were able to give God our best at church. Before we made the decision to do this, it wouldn't take much to cause us to stay home or do something else. Now we never base the choice to go to church on our feelings, the situation, or what we did the night before. The fruit of this has been incredible. Our family has learned to put God first, and we know that His blessings will abound by doing so. Integrity became our guide, and the results were amazing.

"People with integrity do what they say they are going to do. Others have excuses."

Dr. Laura Schlessinger

We form habits of integrity when we live them out day by day, month by month, and year by year. The enemy has no choice but to surrender when he sees people of integrity, for he knows it is useless to try to change their minds. They have set their hearts on it, and eventually, he stops trying. Without integrity, it leaves room for the enemy to maneuver in our lives because we leave too many options on the table of decision.

> *"...but the perversity of the treacherous destroys them."*
> Proverbs 11:3b

The word, treacherous, means to be faithless. The integrity of the heart leads a faithful person to success. A faithless person flounders from one day to the next, struggling to make the right decisions, which hinders their success. If you have integrity, it is a guide to life. One never needs to look too far or hard to do the right thing when integrity is involved.

THINK ON THIS... Do you make decisions based on circumstances or situations, or have you established life-guiding pre-sets of integrity?

WEEK 4 - THE SLUGGARD

Day 16

> I went by the field of the lazy man, And by the vineyard of the man devoid of understanding; And there it was, all overgrown with thorns; Its surface was covered with nettles; Its stone wall was broken down. When I saw it, I considered it well; I looked on it and received instruction: A little sleep, a little slumber, A little folding of the hands to rest; So shall your poverty come like a prowler, and your need like an armed man.
>
> Proverbs 24:30-34

The problem with laziness is that eventually, it manifests in all the areas of our lives that matter. In this Parable, it was quite evident that slothfulness caused the poor condition of the man's vineyard. It was in shambles, overgrown with weeds, and in general disrepair. A vineyard produces grapes, and good quality grapes produce great tasting wines. If the vineyard is neglected, do you think the quality of the grapes will suffer? Then, of course, so does the wine, and when that happens, sales will dwindle. In fact, the writer goes on to explain that when one neglects their business, poverty is right around the corner. Laziness is described as a prowler that will eventually pounce on you and rob you. It will attack powerfully like an armed warrior, strong and mighty. Laziness invites trouble into our lives and must be avoided. It is an issue we need to be extremely cautious about as it has the insidious power to bring a detrimental effect on our lives. What do you want your life to be like? Do you want success or failure, wealth, or poverty, have or have not? Be lazy and you'll end up in poverty. It's totally up to you.

"Without hard work, nothing grows but weeds."
Gordon H. Hinckley

THINK ON THIS... Are there areas in your life that have fallen prey to laziness? What can you do to change those things?

WEEK 4
THE SLUGGARD

Day 17

Despite their desires, the lazy will come to ruin,
for their hands refuse to work.

Proverbs 21:25 NLT

Have you ever asked God for money? In my early days as a Christian, I remember needing X amount of dollars for a fishing trip my brother and I had planned. I didn't have the funds to go, so I prayed. Every day I looked in the mailbox to see if money had supernaturally appeared, but, alas, nothing came. I kept praying, believing that God would somehow supply, as I knew He could. About a week before the trip, I got a call from a friend's dad asking if I could re-shingle his house. We agreed on the amount I would be paid, and I went to work. Once I completed the job, not only did he pay what we agreed upon, but he threw in a bonus, which coincidentally added up to the amount I had prayed for. It's funny because I was looking for God to provide for me supernaturally; I just didn't think it would require anything on my part. Was I ever wrong! He did answer supernaturally, and all I had to do was work. By the way, this sort of thing happened to me over and over. I would pray for money, and I'd get a job offer. It took some time for me to realize that while God could've simply put money into my bank account or sent a cheque, He used the avenue of work to supply my desires. It was supernatural because He provided the answer, but I had to labour to receive it. Had I become stubborn and decided that I wanted God to provide by another method, I wouldn't have received the money. The desire for God to supply was there, but if I refused to work, I would fall short. I learned the valuable lesson that God not only supplied my needs but worked on my character as well.

> *"The reason a lot of people do not recognize opportunity is because it usually goes around wearing overalls looking like hard work."*
>
> Thomas A. Edison

THINK ON THIS... How hard are you willing to work to see your dreams accomplished?

WEEK 4
THE SLUGGARD

Day 18

Laziness casts one into a deep sleep,
and an idle person will suffer hunger.

Proverbs 9:15

The definition of idle is to spend time doing nothing, without purpose and effect.

You only get out of life what you put into it. This is called the law of sowing and reaping. Nothing times nothing equals nothing!

When I attended Bible College many years ago, one of our assignments was to keep track of everything we did for one week. The purpose of this was to bring awareness to what we actually did with our time. Our excuses for not completing homework assignments were likely the impetus behind this exercise. After a week, I realized that I had a considerable amount of idleness in my life. It was extremely enlightening and beneficial to discover I had much more time available and wasn't using it to my advantage. What could we accomplish if we effectively utilize all the time we have? Ask the average person, *"What are you going to do this weekend?"* Nothing is probably the answer you will receive most times. Now you and I both know what they mean. They want to relax after a hard week's work, which is okay for a little while, but the problem is that many people are merely idling away their lives when they could be achieving so much more. Yes, there is a time to rest, recuperate, and gain energy back, but most people overdo it. We don't need to rest so much.

"Folks who never do any more than they get paid for, never get paid for any more than they do."
Elbert Hubbard

Sitting idle for too long will create problems in our lives. If idleness is allowed to grow and dominate our lives, it will lead to lack, hunger, and even ruin. Even our minds will suffer from inactivity. Have you ever heard this Scripture? *"Idle hands are the devil's workshop."* You get the idea. It's better to be busy than to allow our minds to be tempted to think things that are improper, untrue, or non-productive.

THINK ON THIS... How much time do you sit idle in any given week? Can you accomplish more? You won't know until you try.

WEEK 4
THE SLUGGARD

Day 19

The lazy man says, "There is a lion outside!
I shall be slain in the streets!"

Proverbs 22:13

Excuses, excuses, excuses! The sluggard never seems to run out of them. There's always a good reason why they can't help, get involved, or do something they should. It's too cold; it's too hot; it's raining or snowing. The sun is too bright, or it's too dark. Excuses are simply attempts to justify their weak flesh. Some folks always have a reason why they can't do something right now. Later is better for some reason. A quote from Aaron Burr, *"Never do today what you can put off till tomorrow,"* is their motto. Endless excuses will never bring about success in your life. Another name for laziness is procrastination. The procrastinator will try to put off for tomorrow what they could have done today.

> *"My advice is to never do tomorrow what you can do today. Procrastination is the thief of time."*
>
> Charles Dickens

I laugh as I remember when my wife and I asked our children to do chores or things that needed to be done around the house. They would often try to reason with us as to why today wasn't the right time for it. Can't we do it tomorrow? Does it have to be done today? It would be so much better if we could do it on another day. We already have this to do, so there's no point wasting energy on that today. We can clean our rooms tomorrow because we'll do a better job of it then.

Apparently, "now" was a foreign concept to them, and tomorrow was a much better time. Later, Dad! Later, Mom! Everything was destined to be done later. But, if you know my wife, you also know that wasn't happening in our house, and I'm thankful that she instilled in our children to do things now, with no excuses.

There is no time like the present! If you can get it done today, then make it so! Don't allow the "lazy" in you to dictate and control your life. Instead of finding excuses why you can't, look for a great reason why you can. Your life will be better for it!

THINK ON THIS... Do you like to put off till tomorrow what you can do today? Are you a procrastinator, and if so, why?

WEEK 4
THE SLUGGARD

Day 20

Because of laziness the building decays,
and through idleness of hands the house leaks.
Ecclesiastes 10:18

One time I watched an episode of *"American Pickers,"* where they were invited to an estate someone had purchased in an auction. On the property there were various buildings, barns, and a once beautiful house. Because it was left unattended for ten to fifteen years, water had gained access, and it was a mess. The floors were rotting, mold abounded, and this gorgeous building was falling apart. The owner, a very successful contractor, had passed away, and for some reason, it was left as is. Everything in the house was there, but in a deplorable condition. Although not the previous owner's fault, this was the result of neglect.

> *"Success isn't always about greatness. It's about consistency. Consistent hard work leads to success. Greatness will come."*
>
> Dwayne "The Rock" Johnson

Laziness or idleness produces the same result in life. It doesn't matter what grand or majestic buildings we erect, or the things we accomplish, if we, through laziness, allow them to fall to pieces and decay. Maintaining what we have built is as important as creating it in the first place. Another word for maintaining is stewardship. We all have the task to be good stewards of what we possess. And - it's far more cost-effective to keep things properly maintained than it is to rebuild or purchase new. The same goes for everything we do in life. Businesses, ministries, careers, or any organization must be maintained to remain successful and useful. We dare not become indifferent or lose our motivation after the fact.

This is also the case in our spiritual lives. Do we maintain our relationship with the Lord? Do we pray, worship, read our Bibles, participate in church?

How about marriage, children, friends, or family? It applies to everything in life and can cause issues if we allow it. Everything God has given us, be it material, spiritual, or relational, cannot be taken for granted or neglected through laziness. Let's be good stewards of all that we have achieved or been given.

THINK ON THIS...

Do you have areas in your life that need maintenance?

WEEK 5 – THE ART OF LISTENING

Day 21

A wise man will listen and increase his learning and a discerning man will obtain guidance.

Proverbs 1:5

Listening is not the same thing as hearing! It's easy to hear, but not fully grasp what is said. Listening is incredibly more valuable than speaking. It's incredible what we can learn if we really listen. It's not by accident that God created people with two ears and only one mouth. He expects us to listen at least twice as much as we talk; however, I think most of us have that backwards. The trouble with not developing our ability to listen is that we can't learn anything.

When a person is trying to make a point, this can be extremely frustrating for them. One of the best illustrations of this is found in the context of marriage. How often do we find ourselves hearing what the other is saying but not understanding what they mean? We may hear their words, but are we comprehending them? Truth can be discerned if we give our undivided attention to the one speaking. Here's a great example of something I've done in my marriage. I say, *"Honey, I'm going out with some guys tonight."* She replies, *"Oh, ok, I'm going to stay home and relax."* I say, *"Ok, see you later."* Now, let's decipher that conversation. If I only hear but don't listen, I could miss out on what she was trying to communicate to me. What she really meant was, *"I'm staying home to relax, and I sure wish you would stay with me."*

> *"Most people do not listen with the intent to understand; they listen with the intent to reply."*
>
> Stephen R. Covey

I know, I know, we aren't mind readers, but that's life. We do it all the time. Now, if I had applied what I call *"the art of listening,"* I'd have readily discerned her meaning. Love and common sense would have guided me to stay home with her instead of going out.

It's vital that we learn to listen with sensitivity, for that's what the "art of listening" is all about. Hear the words, but also hear what's "behind" the words. Learn to listen carefully, with understanding and wisdom.

THINK ON THIS...

Are you a good listener?

WEEK 5
THE ART OF LISTENING

Day 22

Hear instruction and be wise, and do not disdain it.
Proverbs 8:33

Years ago, my brothers and I loved to play video games whenever we got together. We would rent the games and spend the whole weekend with a controller in our hands, getting the most out of our hard-earned money. Before we played, the instructions were consulted. My brothers would scan them quickly and immediately begin playing, but I always took the time to read them thoroughly. They felt they had the advantage by starting the game before me. After losing time and time again, they realized they were sadly mistaken. Why? Instructions, instructions, instructions! My motto was, why learn from your mistakes when you can understand and do it correctly from the very beginning. The whole point of having the instructions is to learn to play correctly. If we don't read or hear them, how can we succeed? Yes, we will eventually learn through trial and error, but is that the best way? Of course not. Do you think that the people who invented the game also know how to play it to win? That's why they sent the instructions in the first place.

"When all else fails, read the instructions."
Agnes Allen

Learning to win at video games is undoubtedly a far cry from learning how to succeed in life. However, what is true in a game is also true in life. Holy men of God, through the inspiration of the Holy Spirit, wrote what is commonly referred to as the "Bible."

God, who created humanity, gave us this instruction manual to understand how to play the game of life and win.

I must confess that I refused to follow good instruction early in my life, both from my parents and from the Bible. I followed the self-defeating philosophy of the old Frank Sinatra song, *"I Did it My Way,"* and it cost me a great deal. My life went downhill very quickly and only changed direction and course when Jesus found me and saved me from myself. When salvation came, I began to hear instruction. It's mind-boggling how much more open we are to hear directions after making a mess of things. It's like when we put a BBQ together without first reading the instructions and then discover that nothing fits together as it should, and there's leftover pieces. What follows next usually sounds like this from my wife, *"Well, did you read the manual?"*

"A wise person will listen and take in more instruction."
Solomon, Proverbs 1:5

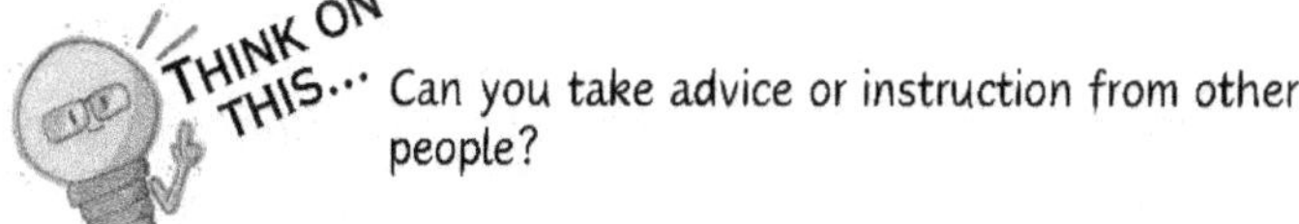

Can you take advice or instruction from other people?

WEEK 5
THE ART OF LISTENING

Day 23

Listen, my son, and be wise;
keep your mind on the right course.
Proverbs 23:19 HCBS

This verse is planted right smack dab in the middle of the author's admonition to avoid gluttony, drunkenness, and adulterous women, as all three lead to poverty and shame. Unfortunately, many people disregard this wise counsel and fall short of the right course for their life. If you want to be wise, you first must "listen." It's like when my children were young, and I would ask them to do something. Even though they heard me, it never got accomplished. I would sometimes sit them down and lecture them on the idea of listening, and while I was speaking, they would say, *"I was listening."* I would counter with, *"If you were listening, why isn't it done?"*

The truth is that while we are always hearing, we aren't always listening. Listening means doing what you hear. As the Scripture says in James 1:22, *"Be doers of the Word and not hearers only."* It's easy to believe we've listened when we have only heard.

"Well done is better than well said."
Benjamin Franklin

"He who has ears to hear, let him be hearing," is an insightful phrase Jesus would often speak to His hearers. He was saying that even though we have ears and hear what another is saying, it doesn't mean we are responding to it with the right course of

action. It's vital that we not only hear the Word of God but take the time to think about it daily, so we can keep ourselves in our right minds and walk in the ways of God as He has commanded. As we do, we will gain valuable knowledge and wisdom to keep out of sin and follow His plan for our lives. The results will speak for themselves.

THINK ON THIS... Are you on the right course? Have you listened to the Word of God or the people He has surrounded you with? Be wise!

WEEK 5
THE ART OF LISTENING

Day 24

A wicked person listens to malicious talk; a liar pays attention to a destructive tongue.

Proverbs 17:4 HCSB

Evil people relish malicious conversation;
the ears of liars itch for dirty gossip.

Proverbs 17:4 Message

I once heard that you could forecast what a person will be like in five years by three things they do now; what they read, who they associate with, and what they listen to. I know this to be true because I've seen many good people corrupted because they were unable to "not" listen to falsehoods, rumours, and gossip. Too many folks love to hear gossip about other people or intently listen when others are maligned or slandered. If you hear people talking improperly about others, do you join in, or do you set them straight? Or, at the very least, do you tell them you won't take part in these character assassinations? When we aren't discerning in what we hear, it becomes extremely easy to take part in malicious talk without realizing it. We must be ever vigilant to stay out of these conversations. Our ears are not garbage cans! God never gave them to us to hear junk. Even the most innocent-sounding gossip has the power to affect us negatively, and we begin to think badly about people because of it. Remember, just because someone said it, or you thought it doesn't make it true.

"One of the most expensive things you can do is to listen to the wrong people."

Dr. Henry Cloud

Doesn't the Bible say that *"love covers a multitude of sins?"* Gossip and malicious talk are like tender morsels that easily go down to the innermost parts of our heart. It's possible to become hard-hearted toward certain individuals simply because we heard something negative about them. It's vital that we carefully monitor what we hear, listen to, and read. We are affected by it, whether we realize it or not.

THINK ON THIS... What do you want to be like in five years? It could all depend on who or what you listen to. Take inventory of the people you associate with. Are they good for you? Really?

WEEK 5
THE ART OF LISTENING

Day 25

To one who listens, valid criticism is like a gold
earring or other gold jewelry.

Proverbs 25:12 NLT

A beautiful woman who rejects good sense is like
a gold ring in a pig's snout.

Proverbs 11:22 HCSB

In both of these references to wearing jewelry, one depicts beauty, while the other does not. The one who hears valid criticism and receives it can wear it like a valuable ornament. Let's be honest, most of us don't like to be criticized, do we? However, there is a distinct difference between a valid critique and simply being criticized. One is beneficial; the other is not. Suppose we are oversensitive, insecure, or have identity struggles in our lives. In that case, we may not be able to grasp the difference and view all criticism as an affront.

Jewelry is designed to accent the wearer's beauty, and when done correctly, it is attractive. For instance, when my wife wears jewelry, it enhances her natural beauty. When we listen to reasonable criticism, it will make our lives beautiful.

On the flip side, when we reject sound criticism, Proverbs' writer compares it to a gold ring in a pig's nose. There's something inherently distasteful about fine jewelry worn on an animal that will end up looking like a mess. Even if you dress up a pig, it's still a pig. Jewelry worn by a pig is like the one who won't receive rational criticism. It doesn't belong, and it's not to be celebrated or beautified.

"The trouble with most of us is that we'd rather be ruined by praise than saved by criticism."

Norman Vincent Peale

If you can receive criticism, you deserve to wear that as you would a gorgeous piece of jewelry. Very few people manage to pull it off, so, when you do, wear it proudly.

THINK ON THIS... How do you react when critiqued? Do you quickly become agitated and offended, or do you think about what was said. Is there truth to it, and can you learn from it?

WEEK 6 – YOUR HEART

Day 26

Guard your heart above all else, for it is the source of life.
Proverbs 4:23 HCSB

When God speaks about the heart, is He referring to that blood-pumping organ in the midst of our chest? No, in reality, He is talking about man's spirit or the inner man – the real person. Man is a spirit. He lives in a body and has a soul - the will, intellect, emotions, and imagination. The "spirit" part of humanity must be protected with all diligence because the source of life flows from it. This means that the heart plays an essential and vital role in our lives and determines whether we are happy or not. Believe it or not, you have the power within to bring out good or evil, and it all originates within your spirit. For instance, a person could allow bitterness to grow in their heart because of hurt caused by what someone else said or did. If allowed to fester, that hurt will eventually manifest itself in anger, bitterness, and even hate.

> *"Keep love in your heart. A life without it is like a sunless garden when the flowers are dead."*
>
> Oscar Wilde

Conversely, just as negative emotions affect the heart and grow within it, so can the positive. It all depends on what we allow into our hearts. That's why the Proverbs exhort us to carefully guard our hearts, for it is a prime place for the germination and growth of life's issues, both good and evil. The heart acts like a sponge, soaking up anything given to it. Therefore, we must take great care to protect it. The heart can be a powerful source of good or the producer of evil; it all depends on what it's subjected to. Please do yourself a favour and guard it diligently! Take heed of what you look at and be aware of what you hear; both affect the heart's condition. Your heart is not a garbage dump! Treat it with great care.

THINK ON THIS... Are you looking after your heart? It is similar to a garden and must receive constant care and attention, lest the weeds take over.

WEEK 6
YOUR HEART

Day 27

> My son, give attention to my words; Incline your ear to my sayings. Do not let them depart from your eyes; Keep them in the midst of your heart; For they are life to those who find them, And health to all their flesh.
>
> Proverbs 4:20–22

There isn't a more powerful force in the universe than when the Word of God is allowed to germinate and produce in a person's heart. God encourages us to keep His Words in the "midst" of our hearts. Those same words will transform from writing on a page to life and health in our bodies when we do. The heart has within it the ability to produce healing power if given the right information to use. So how do we give it the correct information?

1. Pay attention to the Word of God.
2. Listen closely to it.
3. Always keep God's Word in front of our eyes.

As we do these things, those same words will move from our heads into our hearts. The distance between life and death is sometimes only about twelve inches.

When I was a new believer, I struggled mightily with my faults and failures, so much so that if I made a mistake, I would berate myself over and over. I thought that if I could whip myself, so to speak, eventually, God would forgive me. Usually, this process lasted about a month before I started to feel good about myself again. In this way, I was not unlike Martin Luther, who supposedly beat himself on the back with a stick trying to overcome his perceived lack of righteousness.

> *"Even the righteous man is just a sinner living in between sins."*
>
> Eric Jerome Dickey

When I attended Bible College, the Dean, Dr. Pierce, encouraged us to take 3 x 5 recipe cards, write Scriptures on them, and read them regularly. One day, while out walking, I took the card out and read 2 Corinthians 5:21, *"For He was made to be sin, who knew no sin, that we might become the righteousness of God in Christ."* At that very moment, I had a revelation that I was righteous before God, not on my merit, but by His. The Word of God took a twelve-inch journey from my brain to my heart and became life to me. I was able to forgive myself quickly and move on with life. The transition from condemnation to righteousness no longer took weeks or months. It continued to grow shorter and shorter as time went by. Today, over thirty-eight years later, I can receive forgiveness and righteousness very quickly, thanks to God's wonderful and awesome Word.

THINK ON THIS... Are you keeping God's Word close to your heart? Are you reading it everyday? The Bible will be of no benefit laying on a coffee table or unopened in an app on your phone.

WEEK 6
YOUR HEART

Day 28

Anxiety in a man's heart weighs it down,
but a good word cheers it up.

Proverbs 12:25 HCSB

Everyone faces anxiety from time to time, but chronic anxiety can interfere with the quality of your life. While perhaps most recognized for behavioural changes, it can also cause severe consequences to your physical health.

Anxiety is a part of life, but we need to learn how to master it. One way to do that is to hear a good word. Sometimes, that's all it takes to get us out of the doldrums of life.

"A word fitly spoken is like apples of gold in settings of silver."

Proverbs 25:11

"The right word at the right time is like a custom-made piece of jewelry."

Proverbs 25:11 Message

The heart can be quickly influenced by negative words, circumstances, and the situations of life, but an encouraging word can counter its horrible effects. It's very easy to become discouraged or even depressed, and we all need people who will speak good things to help us stay on top.

"Do not anticipate trouble or worry about what may never happen. Keep in the sunlight."

Benjamin Franklin

Another way we can overcome anxiety and worry is to get into the Word of God and allow it to speak to us. I'm amazed at how many times I've read the Bible, and it changed the state of my heart and emotions. I am also grateful for the people who have spoken a fitting word at the right time and helped me stand up just a little straighter. When your spirit is stooped, find a good word!

THINK ON THIS... *The next time you experience anxiety, open the good book and let the Son shine in.*

WEEK 6
YOUR HEART

Day 29

Don't let your heart envy sinners; instead,
always fear the Lord.

Proverbs 23:17 HCSB

Have you ever looked at someone else's life and thought to yourself, *"I wish I had what they have. I wish I could be what they are."* Maybe you've even wished you could be them. Don't worry, that's not envy; that's just a waste of good energy and time. Envy is one of the seven deadly sins and occurs when we become angry and resentful over another's good fortune. It's one thing to admire what others have done or possess, but quite another to become angry and bitter over it. Envy is pure poison and something we don't want anywhere near our hearts. *"Guard your heart with all diligence"* is the advice of Solomon, the writer of Proverbs, and we must take this admonition seriously.

> *"Envy is like drinking poison and waiting for the other person to die."*
>
> Unknown

How destructive is envy? I'm glad you asked. Do you remember the story of Cain and Abel in the Book of Genesis? They both brought an offering to the Lord. Cain's was from the fruit of the land, while Abel brought the firstling of his flock. God accepted Abel's offering but rejected Cain's. This made Cain furious, and the Lord inquired of him, *"Why are you so angry and why has your countenance fallen? If you do well, will you not be accepted?... sin (envy) is lurking at the door; its desire is for you, but you must master it."* The next day Cain killed Abel, and for what reason? Pure envy. Instead of listening carefully to the Word of the Lord, Cain ignored the advice and allowed his heart to become affected. As a result of his evil heart, he murdered his brother. Really? His own brother! All because of envy. If Cain had respected the Lord more than his hurt feelings, he would never have done this dirty deed. As a result, the earth was cursed for Cain and would never grow again the way he wanted it to - a terrible recompense for a green thumb. Envy is not worth it. We never need to allow it because God is more than (Abel) to bless us all. See what I did there? Ha-ha.

THINK ON THIS... Are you content with what you have and who you are?

WEEK 6
YOUR HEART

Day 30

Trust in the Lord with all your heart,
and do not rely on your own understanding;
Proverbs 3:5 HCSB

Faith, at its core, is simply trusting in the Lord with all your heart and soul. It is believing in our great God more than we believe our own feeble reasoning. Far too often, the sound of reason is the only voice to which we listen. I like what Jesus once asked His disciples, *"Why are you reasoning in your hearts?"*

God isn't asking us to figure it all out. Rather, He is asking us to believe in Him. Our personal understanding of life is not to be trusted. Instead, the Proverbs exhort us to fully put our faith in God, who is more than able to do exceedingly, abundantly, above all we can think or ask. There is nothing too difficult for God, and no mountain He cannot move. God is greater than our fears. He is stronger than our doubts and more powerful than any circumstances we may face.

"Pray, and let God worry."

Martin Luther

If we try to figure everything out by our own wisdom, knowledge, or reasoning power, we can quickly lose our trust in God. Jesus never asked His disciples to figure everything out, but only to follow His lead. When we place our trust entirely in the Lord, we don't have to understand everything - the whys, the what's, the where's, etc. Those are God's problems. All He asks us to do is trust Him with ALL our heart and leave room for nothing else. All - everyone knows what "all" means, right? In this case, it means we must keep out anything that would try to compete with the faith of God in our hearts by whatever means necessary. No doubt, no unbelief, wondering, worry, and definitely, no reasoning! All is ALL! It's as simple as that.

Faith's Acronym:

F – Forsaking
A – All
I – I
T – Trust
H – Him

THINK ON THIS... Are you trusting in the Lord with all your heart? What is the position of your heart right now? Is it fixed on God or on your own abilities?

WEEK 7 – TREASURE

Day 31

I rejoice over Your promise like
one who finds vast treasure.
Psalm 119:162 HCSB

The Curse of Oak Island; have you ever heard of it? The last time I saw this reality show, it had been on the air for seven years already. It's all about finding buried treasure. They call it a curse because five or six people have died trying to find the treasure. The two brothers heading up the latest hunt on this supposedly cursed island have spent millions of dollars so far, but the grand total is much greater. Why do people go to such impossible lengths? It's simple. They want the treasure. X marks the spot, and if they can only find it, they will be rich! But...yes, there's always a "but." You see, there's a price to pay to find treasure. Why? Because it's always buried or hidden in a hard-to-find location. Why can't treasure be found out in the open somewhere on the surface? But noooo, that never happens. If you want to find a treasure, you will have to get a shovel and dig.

> *"To what greater inspiration and counsel can we turn than to the imperishable truth found in this treasure house, the Bible?"*
>
> Queen Elizabeth 2

In this passage, the Word of God is compared to a treasure. His promises must be treated like a great and hidden treasure. Although the Bible is the most printed book in history, many have never discovered its hidden gems. For that, one must dig deep within it to find them, but when they do, whoa, it's like finding Blackbeard's treasure chest of gold. God's promises are worth far more than gold and silver, or money that will soon perish. It will never pass away. It will work for us throughout all eternity. It is like gold tried in a furnace seven times. The value is beyond mortal description.

> *"Instruction from Your lips is better for me than thousands of gold and silver pieces."*
>
> Psalm 119:72 HCSB

Unfortunately, the Bible remains unopened and unused by most people. If they only knew the incredible, life-giving power of the Word of God, they would never let the dust settle on it.

THINK ON THIS... How do you treat God's Word? Is it a valuable treasure to you?

WEEK 7
TREASURE

Day 32

Treasures of wickedness profit nothing,
but righteousness delivers from death.

Proverbs 10:2

For where your treasure is, there your heart will be also.

Luke 12:34

It makes sense, doesn't it? The thing a person treasures will be where they place the majority of their time and energy. This provides incredible insight into what a person really and truly loves, even if they proclaim otherwise.

This verse from Luke sums up what Jesus said as He addressed the topic of what life is really about. Jesus was challenging the 1st century crowd to look at who they were actually serving, what they were doing, and why. In His initial discourse, He challenged their hypocrisy. People were saying one thing but doing another, and it was very obvious to Him.

How can we tell if we're hypocritical? Do our lives line up with our words? While we boldly proclaim our love and devotion to God, are we living it out? It's easy to discern by merely looking at what we treasure, for what we value is where our devotion will lie. If we treasure God's presence, then we will be in prayer, worship, and the Word. If we love what God loves, we will be about His business. If, on the other hand, we treasure our lives, hobbies, pursuits, etc., that too will be quickly revealed. It cannot be hidden from the *"eyes of the One with whom we must give account"* (Hebrews 4:13).

What do you spend your time and effort working toward? Presumably, we exert the most effort to obtain whatever we think will bring us the most happiness. It would be a great tragedy to spend your life looking for a hidden treasure, only to find it and discover that it did not bring the happiness you were hoping for!

The good news is that we can take a long, hard look at what we spend our time on and easily figure out if our hearts match our devotion to the Lord. After all, God already knows. The problem is this; do you recognize it? Jesus has given us an incredible plumb line by which we can measure our lives to see if they match up to the Word of God.

> *"So is he who lays up treasure for himself, and is not rich toward God."*
>
> Jesus Christ, Luke 12:21

THINK ON THIS...

What do you treasure most of all in life?

WEEK 7
TREASURE

Day 33

My son, keep my words,
and treasure my commands within you.
Proverbs 7:1

Perhaps the one thing you need to do is make the Word of God your treasure. You may not realize it, but God's Word is more than a guidebook for life. The Bible is a book of seeds. Each word in it has the potential to produce fruit in your life - thirty, sixty, and even a hundred-fold. It is a light that illuminates the path we follow, and it's a lamp that brightens our days. If we value the Word and let it get into our hearts, its treasure is endless. Nothing can compare to it! The Word of God can heal, deliver, and liberate us from all that binds us. It has the power to forgive and cleanse us from all sin and unrighteousness. When the evil of this world defiles us, His Word has the ability to clean us up. When the Word becomes a treasure to us, all things become possible. What you thought was in the realm of the impossible now becomes possible. The Word is not bound; it has no limits and cannot be restrained. Anyone who will believe it enough to read, meditate, and speak out its great and priceless treasures, will soon be rewarded with a multiplied harvest. But to reap these grandiose rewards, it must become the greatest treasure in your life. It must be the first thing you look at when you wake and the last thing before you sleep. If it is truly your treasure, your heart will be in it, after it, and long for it.

"We must allow the Word of God to confront us, to disturb our security, to undermine our complacency and to overthrow our patterns of thought and behaviour."

John Stott

THINK ON THIS... Do you treasure God's Word? Matthew 4:4 says, 'Man shall not live by bread alone, but by every Word that proceeds from the mouth of God.'

WEEK 7
TREASURE

Day 34

Again, the kingdom of heaven is like treasure hidden in a field, which a man found and hid; and for joy over it he goes and sells all that he has and buys that field.

Matthew 13:44

Treasure – what would you give to obtain it? After finding treasure in a field, this man immediately sold all he had to procure the funds necessary to purchase the property. Once he owned it, he could freely enjoy the treasure at his leisure.

"The seeking of the Kingdom of God is the chief business of the Christian life."

A.W. Tozer

Jesus likened this great treasure to the Kingdom of Heaven. If a man sacrifices everything to gain an earthly treasure, how much value should we put on the heavenly one? What is the Kingdom of Heaven worth to you? The problem is that for so many, the reward doesn't seem to fit the price. Jesus often used terms in His teaching like, *"Give it all, give it up, let it go, all that he has, give up your life,"* and so on. The great thing is that when a person pays full price for the Kingdom of Heaven, the rewards and benefits are more than worth it. How much is this Kingdom worth anyway? It's absolutely worth the sticker price, and much more. It is the greatest treasure you will ever find. What will you give to purchase it, and what will you pay to keep it? By the way, there is no such thing as full kingdom value for half price. To get the most out of the Kingdom of Heaven, you must pay the total price. We are told that if a person gives it all up for Jesus and His Kingdom, he will receive a hundredfold, not only in this life but also in the next.

THINK ON THIS... What are you willing to give up or pay to inherit the Kingdom of Heaven? It's costly to follow Jesus, but what is your stopping point? Are you ready to sell out for Jesus?

WEEK 7
TREASURE

Day 35

Then He spoke a parable to them, saying: "The ground of a certain rich man yielded plentifully. And he thought within himself, saying, 'What shall I do, since I have no room to store my crops?' So he said, 'I will do this: I will pull down my barns and build greater, and there I will store all my crops and my goods. And I will say to my soul, "Soul, you have many goods laid up for many years; take your ease; eat, drink, and be merry." But God said to him, 'Fool! This night your soul will be required of you; then whose will those things be which you have provided?'
"So is he who lays up treasure for himself,
and is not rich toward God."

Luke 12:16–21

If you're wondering why this devotional isn't straight out of the book of Proverbs, it's because I ran out of them as there weren't that many that used the word "treasure." Fortunately, Jesus used parables that do an excellent job of basically describing Proverbs. You may see this here and there throughout these devotions.

This parable discusses what people do with the increase they receive in life. The rich man decided to store his vast amount of goods and live at ease, without a single thought for his soul. God took him to task regarding the wisdom of his plan when his life was required of him. What's the point of all of this when it's of no use to you when you're dead? All your increase will then go to someone else. What's the moral of the story? It's this - use your treasure for the benefit of God and His Kingdom here on the earth, as it's useless if you don't. He says that this will be the same for people who lay up treasure for themselves and not for God. We can increase in many areas of our lives, but if it's only used selfishly, then our scenario will one day be the same as the prosperous farmer. If this happens, God will also call us "foolish." This parable's goal is to redirect our thinking to what's really important in life, and it's not to increase just for the sake of increase. It's to take what we have gained and use it for God, and in this manner, become rich toward God.

> *"No man is rich enough to buy back his past."*
>
> Oscar Wilde

Matthew 6:20 says, *"But lay up for yourselves treasures in heaven, where neither moth nor rust destroys and where thieves do not break in and steal."* In other words, treasures on earth don't have the same intrinsic value as those we store up in heaven. In fact, the treasures of earth will eventually be destroyed in some manner, but only what is done for God will be eternal. Jesus is attempting to get us to understand the value of eternal things. Being rich in God has infinite, everlasting value, as opposed to the material things we accumulate in our natural life. When we use what we have for God's purposes and plans, we will become rich in Him.

THINK ON THIS...

If God were to examine you right now, would He call you rich in goods or rich in God?

WEEK 8 – DISCRETION

Day 36

For teaching shrewdness to the inexperienced,
knowledge and discretion to a young man.
Proverbs 1:4 HCSB

Solomon, the wisest man that ever walked the face of the earth, penned the book of Proverbs in the hope that it would give knowledge to the simple, wisdom to the fool, and discretion to the inexperienced. Experience is a great teacher, but the best one is hearing and obeying the Word of God.

Discretion is a word that's not generally used until an "indiscretion" occurs.

We are willing to forgive your "little indiscretion," is a phrase used to let someone know they did wrong without openly revealing it. It seems that an indiscretion is a wrong action that a person wouldn't normally do. It's a mistake, a fault, a lack of good judgment, a lapse of common sense. You get the idea.

> *"The better part of valour is discretion; in the which better part I have saved my life."*
>
> William Shakespeare

The phrase, *"the better part of valour is discretion,"* means that the best sort of courage, the kind that constitutes true bravery, rather than recklessness, is courage that is guided by discretion. Bravery, applied blindly, without using caution and wisdom, is meaningless and dangerous.

Being courageous at the wrong time can be hazardous to our lives. Discretion is knowing the difference. There are certain times when we need to be very discreet in life.

Of course, I'm not promoting gambling, but this old song by Kenny Rogers says is clearly.

> *"You got to know when to hold 'em, know when to fold 'em, know when to walk away, and know when to run. You never count your money when you're sittin' at the table, there'll be time enough for countin' when the dealin's done."*
>
> The Gambler

Jesus cautioned His followers to be *"shrewd as serpents but harmless as doves."* That sure sounds like discretion to me. Some folks get into trouble simply because they lack discretion. Wise people see the danger and avoid it. The Word of God helps us to be discreet. Read it, learn it, and obey it, and the life you save just might be your own.

THINK ON THIS... Are you learning to be discreet in your dealings? Have you ever learned a lesson from the School of Hard Knocks? Would discretion have saved you a bump on the head?

WEEK 8
DISCRETION

Day 37

The discretion of a man makes him slow to anger,
and his glory is to overlook a transgression.

Proverbs 19:11

I love how the Amplified Bible puts it - *"Good sense makes a man restrain his anger, and it is his glory to overlook a transgression or an offence."*

Discretion is having good or common sense, something that is not so common. Some folks are easily angered and offended. They are constantly at war with someone or something in life. For one reason or another, they are angry. A person who lacks discretion will allow themselves to be offended over almost anything. The wise understand the futility of anger and offence and refuse to be baited. In the book of James, we are exhorted to *"be slow to anger,"* as anger hardly ever promotes godliness and righteousness.

> *"A wise man is cautious and turns from evil, but a fool is easily angered and is careless."*
>
> Proverbs 14:16 HCSB

An angry person is a careless person. And a careless person will eventually land in hot water. Is it wrong to get angry? No, but it's wrong when we allow anger to override discretion. It's never a good idea to make decisions out of anger, and never, ever, ever, ever confront anyone when you're angry. In fact, doing almost anything in anger is a mistake. The problem with anger is that it easily disregards common sense. When a person sees red, it's tough to give it up. Don't let your temper get the best of you.

> *"If you are patient in one moment of anger, you will escape a hundred days of sorrow."*
>
> Chinese Proverb

Solomon takes this point one step higher by teaching us that when we disregard an offence, even if it incites anger, it is something to be proud of. To overlook anger and offence is to be like God, who has done this for all humanity. He hasn't treated us as we deserve but has shown us incredible mercy and grace. He puts away His anger because of the sacrifice on the cross of His Son, Jesus; and calls us righteous. While His anger is always justified, ours is not!

Anger can open the door wide and give the enemy a foothold in your life. Give up anger and offence and shut the door. Learn to become unoffendable.

WEEK 8
DISCRETION

Day 38

A good man deals graciously and lends;
He will guide his affairs with discretion.

Psalm 112:5

When the Bible speaks of a "good man," it is usually talking about one who loves God, wants to do good for others, and generally be wise in all his dealings. Discretion is the ability to guide our lives in every area according to what is just, right, and fair. One of the ways by which we can walk discreetly is to treat others with grace and mercy. Mercy triumphs over judgment. Some folks live life out of judgment; others live with grace. Judgmental people are quick to point out the shortcomings and faults of others, indict them for their sins, and are generally hard on everyone, expecting perfection from them. On the other hand, people who deal with grace are quick to forgive, cover up offences, and let others make mistakes; knowing that they themselves are not without fault.

"Judgment is not upon all occasions required, but discretion always is."

Lord Chesterfield

A good man is a giver who looks for ways to benefit others. A person of discretion knows that living a life of giving is the best way to live. Discretion gives us the power to make our own choices. We have the discretion to do as we please. We can use that power to give, or we can use it to withhold. One brings blessing, the other poverty. A person who guides his life with grace and giving, will never go wrong.

THINK ON THIS... The greatest power is not merely the power to choose, but rather, the power to choose the right thing.

WEEK 8
DISCRETION

Day 39

My son, if you accept my words and store up my commands within you... Discretion will watch over you, and understanding will guard you.

Proverbs 2:1,11 HCSB

Growing up, I was a *"jump first and think later"* kind of kid. Thinking always came later, and usually at a price. "*What were you thinking?*" was what I often heard from my parents. My answer was always the same, "*I wasn't thinking.*" Yeah, they'd already figured that out. One time, a friend and I walked all over my hometown and let the air out of all the car tires we could. Not only that, but we also took out the valve stems and kept them. Yes, you read that right. Me, Mr. Stupid, did that. I regret it to this day. And to add injury to insult, my dad, who, after giving me a well-deserved whipping, had to pay for it all. I often wondered why people looked at me funny for a long time.

What did I lack? You got it! Discretion. I would be happy to report that this was the only time I lacked that trait, but unfortunately, it wasn't. I laugh now, but it wasn't quite so funny back in the day when I was reprimanded, punished, or frowned upon by the local authorities. I didn't learn about discretion until after I was a Christian. When the Word of God began to enter that unused gray matter between my ears, it started to take hold and saved my life. Discretion began to watch over me, guard me, and keep me from trouble. I no longer had to live in paranoia, looking over my shoulder; and boy, was it a relief.

"A sound discretion is not so much indicated by never making a mistake as by never repeating it."

Christian Nestell Bovee

THINK ON THIS... We have all committed indiscretions, but have we learned our lesson? Are we learning discretion?

WEEK 8
DISCRETION

Day 40

> Maintain your competence and discretion. My son,
> don't lose sight of them. They will be life for you and
> adornment for your neck. Then you will go safely
> on your way, your foot will not stumble.
> Proverbs 3:21-23 HCSB

How do we maintain our discretion? By keeping God's Word close to us. We are to keep it before our eyes (read it), which then translates into our hearts and minds. When this occurs, we will be able to maintain sound judgment in all our affairs. The reason people can't walk with discretion is because their hearts and minds are not able to process it. An unrenewed mind will think things contrary to discretion. If our minds are not sound, how then can our lives be? Competence in life comes through discretion. And discretion comes through the knowledge of God and the renewal of our minds, thoughts, thinking, and reasoning. If our "Word life" isn't strong, then our ability to act discreetly in life will be weak. The two go hand in hand. You can't have one without the other. Merely wanting to be discreet isn't good enough. We must have our thinking processor renewed and reformed by the Word of God. We can't do what we don't know!

For example, have you ever desired to change the way you talk? I had made enough mistakes with my mouth, and I had to change. Here's what I did early on after I was born again as a new believer in Christ. I wrote out the verse, Ephesians 4:29, and taped it to the mirror in my bathroom. It said, *"Let no corrupt word proceed out of your mouth, but what is good for necessary edification, that it may impart grace to the hearers."*

Every day, I would look at it and read it out loud. Every day, I would leave the house thinking about it. Every day, I became that much closer to my goal. The more I looked at it, the greater the impact it had on my life. Eventually, my speech improved and grew more comparable to that verse. We must never stop reading or looking at the Word of God, as its power is unlimited. Never lose sight of it, as it will keep you from stumbling and safe from self-imposed problems.

> *"The true test of maturity is doing the right thing without being prodded."*
>
> Brent Rudoski

THINK ON THIS... Never lose sight of the Word of God! Read it everyday!

WEEK 9 – RIGHTEOUS

Day 41

The righteous should choose his friends carefully,
For the way of the wicked leads them astray.
Proverbs 12:26

When people miss church or falter in their walk with the Lord, we usually ask the same question, *"Who are they hanging out with?"* It's incredible how often this turns out to be the cause. They have friends with no intention of serving the Lord, or old friends they simply cannot break away from to stay out of trouble.

Friends, to some people, are everything. They would do anything to gain a friend, for they surmise that even a bad friend is better than no friend at all.

When little children play, they make friends so quickly. They might not know each other from a hole in the ground, but as soon as they start playing, suddenly, they become bestest of buddies.

There is something wonderful and special about having really good friends in our lives. We all need a good friend from time to time, don't we? But what we don't need are friends who are not good for us. What's the big deal? Why can't we be friends with everyone? Because friends have the ultimate power to influence, more so than leaders, family, pastors, teachers, etc.

> *"Do not be so deceived and misled! Evil companionships (communion, associations) corrupt and deprave good manners and morals and character."*
>
> 1 Corinthians 15:33 AMP

Just as iron sharpens iron, evil friendships have the power to corrupt. Whether you realize it or not, your future and destiny are affected by the quality of your friendships. I've known people who have mistakenly used the good, godly character traits of faithfulness and loyalty in the wrong context to stay true to their ungodly friends. In the end, it hurt them greatly. Sometimes, in life, we must wean ourselves from certain friends if they are negatively affecting us.

Associate yourself with people of good quality, for it is better to be alone than in bad company.

> *"I once had a good friend, who was at one time my employer, and then became my friend. I witnessed to him at the beginning of our relationship, and he would listen, but as time went by, he became increasingly hostile to the words I spoke to him about God. I had no choice but to stay silent as far as God was concerned and be a friend. The problem was that through our close friendship, I was being adversely affected. Instead of influencing him, he was influencing me. As much as it grieved me to do so, I had to gradually wean him off of our friendship. I stopped answering the phone, gave*

excuses why I couldn't hang out, and eventually he was gone out of my life. As much as I liked him, I couldn't afford him in my life. Some folks might have a problem with what I had done, but I knew what would happen if I didn't. You have to pick and choose your friends wisely or run the risk of being led astray."

Booker T. Washington

THINK ON THIS... What kind of friends do you have? Do they serve the Lord and motivate you to do the same? Do they tell you the truth or just what you want to hear? Be honest – are they good for you or not? Choose your friends wisely!

WEEK 9
RIGHTEOUS

Day 42

The Lord is far from the wicked,
But He hears the prayer of the righteous.
Proverbs 15:29

Have you ever thought to yourself, *"God doesn't hear my prayers anymore?"* In life, it's so easy to think along these lines. Everyone has had prayers that seemingly went unanswered. I can't say I understand why that happens, but I do know that if you are righteous, God hears. This verse has always helped me. It encourages me and renews my faith in Him. Isaiah 59:1 says that *"His arms are not short nor is he deaf, that He cannot hear."* God hears prayer. We need to remember that the concept of prayer was not our idea, but His. He instituted prayer, we didn't. God is the God who hears the cries of His people.

The Bible declares, *"He is able to do exceedingly abundantly above all we can ask or think, according to the power that works in us."* The Holy Spirit is always there, helping us pray according to God's will. When we do that, He answers. I've found that my best prayers ensue when I pray until God starts praying through me. When the Holy Spirit prays through you, you can bet donuts to dollars that God answers.

> *"Prayer is not asking, prayer is putting oneself in the hands of God, at His disposition and listening to His voice in the depths of your heart."*
>
> Mother Teresa

Remember that God delights in hearing and answering the prayers of His children. It brings Him glory when we pray in His Son's name. And Jesus teaches us that asking in His name brings powerful results. As we abide in Christ, letting His Word dwell in us, and obeying it to the fullest, God will answer our prayers. Don't let a few unanswered prayers hinder or stop you from seeking God. If you seek Him with all your heart, He will hear you. The enemy of your soul will tell you that you aren't good enough for God to hear you, but that's a bold-faced lie. You are the righteousness of God in Christ. You are good enough, not in yourself, but because of Jesus. That's why we pray in Jesus' name and not in our own. Our name isn't righteous, but His name is. Put your faith in His name and watch what God will do!

THINK ON THIS... Are you genuinely asking in faith and spending time in prayer? Don't let anyone tell you God doesn't hear you because He does. Just make sure you are actually praying.

WEEK 9
RIGHTEOUS

Day 43

The fear of the wicked will come upon him,
and the desire of the righteous will be granted.
Proverbs 10:24

Fear is a terrible tormenter. Its mission is to lie to people and eventually convince them that what they fear will come upon them, and sometimes, it does. Why? Because they believed it. Fear worms its way into the heart of man and can become a reality if allowed to operate. The truth is that most of what we fear will never happen. The best thing we can do with fear is to face it head-on. If we don't, it will continue to torment us.

"The wicked flee when no one pursues, But the righteous are bold as a lion."

Proverbs 28:1

Fear has the insidious power to deceive us into believing life is worse than it actually is. Someone who doesn't have the Lord in their life may struggle with it, but to the righteous, fear has no hold on them because *"God hasn't given us the spirit of fear, but of power, love, and a sound mind."* Therefore, the righteous can act like a lion, fearless and bold. Fear has lost its hold on the righteous!

"The desire to fulfill the purpose for which we were created is a gift from God."

Aiden Wilson Tozer

It says, *"and the desire of the righteous will be granted."* Look at that! God wants to grant the righteous their desires. I can't tell you how many times I've secretly desired for certain things to happen, and they have, without me even praying about them. God caused them to happen. Like the best Father ever, He knows what is in the hearts of His children. After all, He put those desires there in the first place. Once He deposits His desires into our hearts, He goes ahead and fulfills them.

God is a good God, and He does good for His children.

THINK ON THIS... Fear tries to steal your true desires, but you can stop it in its tracks right now. Fear has no place unless you allow it. Overcome fear by trusting in God, for He is greater!

WEEK 9
RIGHTEOUS

Day 44

Righteousness guards people of integrity,
but wickedness undermines the sinner.

Proverbs 13:6 HCSB

Did you ever think that righteousness could be considered a guard over you? Righteousness is called "integrity." Integrity is being honest and faithful. It's acting responsibly - doing what is right even when no one is looking. Another way to look at this is to see wickedness or sin as leaven. According to Galatians 5:9, *"A little leaven leavens the whole lump."* Just as a tiny amount of yeast will eventually permeate the whole batch of dough, wickedness will do the same in a person. Sin ultimately causes trouble and harm to the sinner. It may not seem so at first. It might even be fun for a season, but sin continues to work behind the scenes long after the act is accomplished. Sin undermines the one who sins, for it has no respect of persons, and will bring trouble upon them.

> *"Sin promises more than it delivers, costs you more than you want to pay, and takes you farther than you want to go."*
>
> Unknown

Wickedness can also be compared to rust. Rust works to corrode metal. It starts small, but left unchecked, it can soon rot out an entire car. Sin is to a human as rust is to metal. Sin, if continued, is a cancer that will ultimately cause untold harm and pain. One of the reasons God sent His only begotten Son to die for mankind was to eradicate sin and its effects in our lives.

When God gave the big ten commandments to Moses for Israel, some might've looked at them as obstructions, but in truth, they were a protection against the onslaught of sin's purposes and plans. Sin, in all its forms, is harmful to humanity.

When I was twelve years old, I remember praying to God in my bed. However, it seemed like my prayers were hitting the ceiling and bouncing right back to me. I believed in God, but it seemed like He couldn't be found, so I decided to give up all restraint and go hard, drinking alcohol, doing drugs, etc. It started out as fun but eventually caused me great pain, sorrow, and loss. The end certainly couldn't be seen at the beginning. I found out the hard way that sin doesn't pay good dividends. While I thought I was having fun doing whatever I wanted, it undermined my life right beneath my nose, and I was ignorantly unaware. After ten years of constant partying, drinking, and drug use, my life was shot to rats. I was extremely skinny, worn out, full of fear, anxiety, and paranoia. I began to lose all hope for a bright future, a by-product of my hard living. Thank God that when I wasn't even looking, Jesus found me. Since that time, over thirty-eight years ago, I can say with confidence that righteousness does indeed protect and guard against trouble. Sin brings trouble, but righteousness produces blessings and life.

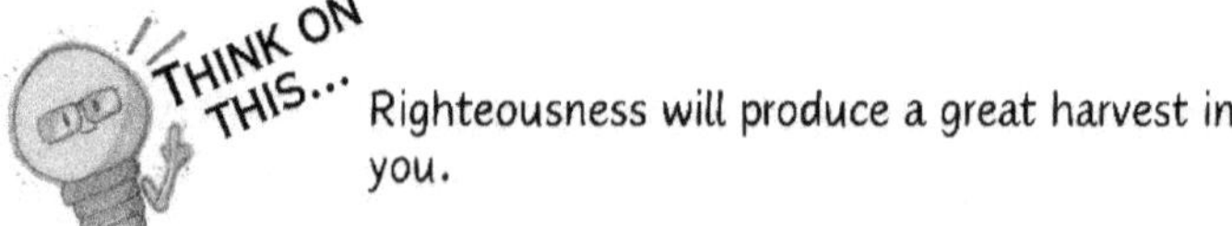

Righteousness will produce a great harvest in you.

WEEK 9
RIGHTEOUS

Day 45

> No weapon formed against you will succeed, and you will refute any accusation raised against you in court. This is the heritage of the Lord's servants, and their righteousness is from Me." This is the Lord's declaration.
>
> Isaiah 54:17 HCSB

The enemy of God is called the "accuser" of the brothers. He uses God's Law to accuse Christians in the same way a prosecuting attorney would. He tries to prosecute them for their sins and shortcomings through accusation and deception. But alas, He cannot because God has already forgiven their sins and caused them to be righteous through the shed blood of Jesus. Suppose the enemy could successfully bring an accusation against the people of God. In that case, he would also believe he has the right to inflict them with punishment, just as God punished him for his rebellion. The difference between fallen angels and us is that we are redeemed, and they are not. They will never be able to understand what Jesus truly did on the cross that day when they thought they had won the victory. Instead, He was victorious as He turned the tables on His enemies. Since that time, Satan has attempted to use the power of accusation to separate the saints from God's love. Fortunately, this is no longer possible because God now defends us from these falsehoods.

> *"The next time Satan reminds you of your past, remind him of his future."*
>
> Carmen

Every time the enemies of God cry out in accusation against us, Jesus' blood cries out, redeemed, sanctified, and innocent of all charges. The charges that are brought against us were nailed on that cross 2,000 years ago. We are no longer guilty, and thereby unrighteous. We are now called the righteousness of God in Christ.

No weapon, that is, no accusation levelled against you will succeed or prosper. The indictment has no legal right to lay hold on you. Hence, all allegations are false and shall not be considered. They are stricken from the record. We must rise up and speak out with boldness when we are accused, saying, *"I am God's righteousness in Christ. Devil, you are a liar, and eventually, you will be a fryer."* Whenever you feel accused or condemned, simply remind yourself of who you now are in Christ and that all the charges were dropped at Calvary. There is no record of wrongs in existence against you because they were all nailed on the cross of Christ.

> *"Who can bring an accusation against God's elect? God is the One who justifies. Who is the one who condemns? Christ Jesus is the One who died, but even more, has been raised; He also is at the right hand of God and intercedes for us."*
>
> Romans 8:33–34 HCSB

THINK ON THIS...

You are the righteousness of God in Christ!

WEEK 10 – EXCELLENCE

Day 46

> Then this Daniel was preferred above the presidents and princes, because an excellent spirit was in him; and the king thought to set him over the whole realm.
>
> Daniel 6:3

Daniel was found to have an excellent spirit. This is an important verse of Scripture as it points to Daniel's source of excellence - his spirit. Everything about him screamed excellence. Everything he did was outstanding. It wasn't just what he did that spoke excellence to those around him, it was also his demeanour and attitude.

The *King James Dictionary* defines excellence as*: "Being of great virtue or worth; eminent or distinguished for what is amiable, valuable or laudable; as an excellent man or citizen; an excellent judge or magistrate."*

In the King's opinion, Daniel was preferred above the others, and as such, was given more authority and responsibility in his kingdom. Another translation puts it this way, *"He was distinguished above his peers."* Makes sense, doesn't it? I mean, if you were going to promote someone, what characteristics would you like to see? Would it be someone who doesn't finish well, comes in late, leaves early, and struggles to do the tasks assigned efficiently? No, of course not. You would look for the spirit or attitude of excellence – a person who showed up on time, worked hard until the end, had a great attitude, worked well with others, and did the common things in an uncommon way. Excellence is doing something common in an uncommon way!

> *"If a man is called to be a street sweeper, he should sweep even as Michelangelo painted, or Beethoven composed music or Shakespeare wrote poetry. He should sweep streets so well that all the hosts of heaven and earth will pause to say, "Here lived a great street sweeper who did his job well.""*
>
> Martin Luther King Jr.

THINK ON THIS... If they were looking to promote someone at your workplace, would they choose you?

WEEK 10
EXCELLENCE

Day 47

Then the presidents and princes sought to find occasion against Daniel concerning the kingdom; but they could find no occasion nor fault; forasmuch as he was faithful, neither was there any error or fault found in him.

Daniel 6:4

Although Daniel's excellent spirit brought him to a higher place and position in the kingdom, it didn't come without backlash. It amazes me how people can be envious of those who get promoted in life. Perhaps it's because an excellent spirit is seen by all and thus, reveals our own shortcomings. If you are of an excellent spirit, you will find promotion but also create enemies. Some folks get irritated when others live a more successful life than their own. It reveals the mediocre life they are living and brings their own lack to the surface - not something they want the world to see. They would rather have everyone live and work at a low level, then it's much easier for them to hide their lack of excellence and still look good enough.

These "leaders" tried extremely hard to find fault with Daniel. I could see them secretly conspiring against him, saying, *"Who is this Hebrew, this foreigner, who acts so uppity, like he's better than the rest of us. Why should he get promoted instead of us? Let's find some dirt on him!"*

"Every job is a self-portrait of the person who did it. Autograph your work with excellence."

Jessica Guidobono

They scrutinized, but could not find; they searched, but to no avail, and found Daniel to be unusually excellent. Could the same be said of us? I hope so.

THINK ON THIS...

Can your life withstand the serious scrutiny of others?

Week 10
Excellence

Day 48

But Daniel, brimming with spirit and intelligence, so completely outclassed the other vice-regents and governors that the king decided to put him in charge of the whole kingdom.

Daniel 6:3 Message

To brim with spirit means overflowing with a great attitude. An excellent spirit is just that - an attitude. It's an attitude, a mindset, a way of thinking and being. It's choosing to be positive when others are negative. It's being happy and joyful when everyone is discouraged or depressed.

It has been said that *"attitude determines altitude,"* and I believe it. Sometimes, the only discernable difference between people is their attitude. If attitude truly determines altitude, you better pick a good one.

Having a proper attitude is a choice, one that we can make every day. People with bad attitudes have the same choice as everyone else. No one is born with a bad attitude; it's learned behaviour. Excellence is not necessarily a skill but an attitude.

"Watch your attitude; it's the first thing people notice about you!"

Author Unknown

Excellence in life starts with understanding the concept of maintaining a great attitude and that doing so will eventually lead to success. People love a good attitude in others and are inexplicably drawn to the person possessing this trait.

THINK ON THIS... How has your attitude been? Take an attitude self-test.

WEEK 10
EXCELLENCE

Day 49

> But Daniel purposed in his heart that he would not defile himself with the portion of the king's meat, nor with the wine which he drank: therefore, he requested of the prince of the eunuchs that he might not defile himself.
>
> Daniel 1:8

Daniel purposed in his heart to be a man of excellence. He had a conviction that this was the way he wanted to live. Too often, in today's world, we see people who don't care at all about how they live, work, behave, etc. As a newly saved twenty-three-year-old, I was hired by a roofing company and given the "wonderful" position of labourer, lackey, and grunt. I basically did everything the roofers didn't want to do - loading, stripping the roof, cleaning, etc. It was hard labour, but I worked at it as if I was doing it for the Lord. I must have done an excellent job because from time to time my boss would secretly give me a raise, along with instructions not to tell the others. Then, as we all gathered every morning in the office, the roofers would offer me more money if I would work for them that day. There were other labourers, but they began to fight over me. Why? Because I worked hard and had a great attitude, they made more money and made it faster. Working with excellence brought prosperity to everyone around me.

I knew nothing about excellence at the time, but I knew that I belonged to the Lord, and I wanted to please Him in all things, which, I guess, translated into the workplace. I remember purposing in my heart to have a great attitude, work harder than anyone else, and enjoy doing it. If we want to be excellent in life, we must have a conviction about it.

In his book, *The Whitehouse Years*, Henry Kissinger tells of a Harvard professor who had given an assignment and was now collecting the papers. He handed them back the next day, and at the bottom of one was written, *"Is this the best you can do?"* The student thought, *"No,"* and redid the paper. It was handed in again and received the same comment. This happened ten more times, until finally, the student said, *"Yes, this is the best I can do."* The professor replied, *"Fine, now I'll read it."*

> *"Excellence is not an accomplishment. It is a spirit, a never-ending process."*
>
> Lawrence M. Miller

I love that. *"Is this the best you can do?"* What a great question, one that we all need to answer.

Here's another question. How is it that you can assign two people the same task and get two different results? One does a great job and the other a so-so job. Why? Excellence of spirit and conviction. Every one of us has the choice to do our very best or be mediocre. Today, I encourage you to determine to do your very best in everything you do. I guarantee that you will be a blessing not only to others but also to yourself if you do.

THINK ON THIS... What can do you to be more excellent? Can you think of any areas where you could do better?

WEEK 10
EXCELLENCE

Day 50

Daniel distinguished himself above the administrators and satraps because he had an extraordinary spirit, so the king planned to set him over the whole realm.

Daniel 6:3 HCSB

Excellence is not perfectionism. I'm not talking about being someone who is in bondage to a neurotic lifestyle where nothing is ever good enough. Don't be a people pleaser. Put in the time, energy, and effort so you can honestly say, *"I did my very best."* That is the difference between being excellent and being a perfectionist.

A perfectionist is one who demands exactness from everybody else, but not always of himself. An excellent person expects the very best he can be at that time. To be excellent, we must walk the walk, not just talk the talk!

Do you care about being excellent, or are you content with just an *"it's ok"* kind of life? What do you want to be like, known for, or become?

Excellence is the way to rise above in any area of life. It has the uncanny ability to get the attention of both God and people like nothing else can. Excellence can be the key that opens the king's door.

"If you want to achieve excellence, you can get there today. As of this second, quit doing less than excellent work."

Thomas J. Watson

Daniel was granted favour with the prince of the eunuchs. How do you suppose he did that? Blinded the man, bribed him, took him out back and gave him a good talking to, or maybe roughed him up a bit. NO! Daniel brought this on by his attitude, his words, and his actions. They all spoke volumes to the prince.

Excellence in life is that one quality that some have, and some don't. It's the difference between a *"that's good enough"* and *"a job well-done"* attitude.

THINK ON THIS... Decide now to stop doing less than excellent work. Today is the day you take your life up a notch.

WEEK 11– HONOUR

Day 51

Before his downfall a man's heart is proud,
but humility comes before honour.
Proverbs 18:12 HCSB

The problem with pride is that it never produces any good in our lives. Humility lifts us up, but pride pulls us down. It would almost seem the other way around. Pride makes one feel lifted up but it's a deception, it's self-raising. A person with pride has honour as their motivation and ambition - they want to be honoured. A humble person has no such aspirations. They don't care about being honoured, it's not their motivation in life.

"A person's pride will humble him, but a humble spirit will gain honour."

Proverbs 29:23 HCSB

Don't be like the guy who, through pride, sought to sit in a place of honour, a high place that wasn't his to take. When the bride and groom saw him sitting where he didn't belong, he was relegated to a lower seat. He would have avoided this embarrassment if he had shown even a little humility.

It's also possible that in the same wedding scenario, someone who deserved a place of honour had humbly chosen a lesser seat. No doubt, the bride and groom would have moved him to a place of higher honour.

This is the way pride and humility work. Pride always brings a downward spiral, while humility causes an upward draft.

"Pride is at the bottom of all great mistakes."

John Ruskin

In Matthew 23:12, Jesus put it like this, *"He who exalts himself will be humbled and he who humbles himself will be exalted."* The trouble with this is that we are much more susceptible to pride than humility. Why? Pride is difficult to discern in our own lives. It's easy to pinpoint in others, but difficult to see in ourselves.

The good news is that even though pride is a definite troublemaker in our lives, we can overcome it. There will be more than enough humbling incidents in our lives that we will be able to learn from. The key is to learn from them. We all make mistakes, but not everyone learns from them.

THINK ON THIS... When your pride is challenged, how do you respond?

Week 11
Honour

Day 52

Uzziah was sixteen years old when he became king,
and he reigned fifty-two years in Jerusalem.
His mother's name was Jecholiah of Jerusalem.
And he did what was right in the sight of the Lord,
according to all that his father Amaziah had done.
He sought God in the days of Zechariah, who had
understanding in the visions of God; and as long as he
sought the Lord, God made him prosper.

2 Chronicles 26:3-5

Yesterday we learned that humility always comes before honour. King Uzziah was a prime example of this. As long as He sought the Lord (humility), God honoured him in everything and prospered all he did.

> *"True humility isn't thinking less of yourself; it is thinking of yourself less."*
>
> Rick Warren

We may have the mistaken idea that to be humble, a person must degrade themselves and allow others to step all over them, but not so. The Bible commands us not to think of ourselves more highly than we ought to, and there is a proper way to do this. We are to think highly of ourselves, but not to the extent of pride. When we become proud, we've gone too far and are thinking more highly than we should.

What comes after pride?

Uzziah was a great king who accomplished incredible things. He built and fortified towers, dug wells, and raised livestock. With God as his help, he raised a great and strong army, outfitted with the latest and greatest in body armour and all manner of weaponry. He designed and built giant catapults to launch huge boulders and set them up on high to powerfully defend the land. He was helped marvellously by God, and his fame spread far and wide because of his humble heart.

> *"But when he was strong his heart was lifted up, to his destruction, for he transgressed against the Lord his God by entering the temple of the Lord to burn incense on the altar of incense."*
>
> 2 Chronicles 26:16

I find it amazing how we can be so humble when we are small and needy, but when we become strong, that humility quickly vanishes. Instead of continuing to realize our success comes from the Lord as we walk humbly with Him, we start to believe we have prospered by our own hand. This is nothing but the devil's work, who is the ultimate example of pride. He, too, desired to be exalted to higher heights but was ultimately cast down and will be brought down even further one day soon.

Unfortunately, Uzziah learned the hard way that pride doesn't pay as he attempted to walk in positions of authority never given to him. Yes, he was the king, but he wasn't a priest of God.

One of the keys to staying humble is to remain in your calling. Don't look at other things because the grass isn't greener on the other side. The grass on your side is precisely what you need!

To make a long story short, when Uzziah tried to burn incense, the priests challenged him, saying, *"Only the priests can offer incense to the Lord. This is not for you. If you continue, the Lord will no longer honour you."* Did he listen? No, his pride blinded him to the truth, and he became enraged at them. While he was offering incense, his flesh became leprous, and he was run out of the temple. He remained a leper until the day he died. I guess he was still the king, but he was isolated from everyone from that day on—what a sad outcome to such a promising beginning.

> *"Once you reach the top, take care as the only way left to go is down."*
>
> Darren Bateman

THINK ON THIS... Strength can be a deception, a pathway for pride. Be careful to stay weak and needy for God – it will be your defence against pride.

WEEK 11
HONOUR

Day 53

Poverty and disgrace come to those who ignore discipline,
but the one who accepts correction will be honoured.
Proverbs 13:18 HCSB

How often have we succumbed to pride when we were corrected, challenged, or admonished? Our pride struggles to listen to others because we don't like to be wrong. As a pastor, I've talked with many people who appeared to listen but ultimately ignored the advice offered. It's usually not long after that I begin hearing of trouble in their lives. If they had only listened to good, solid advice, honour would have been theirs.

Why do we hate to be wrong? What is it about this that causes people to fight for their "rightness?" I've often seen this operate in marriage. For some strange reason, our desire to be right overrides our good sense. We would rather be right than happy.

I believe this desire to be right came to us straight from the Garden of Eden, where both Adam and Eve made excuses and blamed others for their own errors. Adam blamed the woman and God, and the woman blamed the serpent. In their newfound desire to be right, they allowed a wrong to surface. From that point on, it has been the same throughout history. We would rather keep our pride intact by claiming rightness instead of drawing honour to ourselves by humbly accepting when we're wrong.

"When receiving correction, the wise seeks to learn and the fool seeks to justify with excuses."

Kevin Everett FitzMaurice

I have learned, after being challenged or corrected after preaching, to take everything into consideration. At first, I took offence but have since learned to ponder their words. If there is some truth to what they said, I can learn from it. If they are totally out to lunch, I can still learn not to take life too seriously and give them grace. Either way, I win.

THINK ON THIS... How do you respond when your opinions or decisions are challenged? When you receive advice, do you immediately defend your position, or do you listen for the wisdom that may come?

WEEK 11
HONOUR

Day 54

Whoever tends a fig tree will eat its fruit, and whoever looks after his master will be honoured.

Proverbs 27:18 HCSB

I love this proverb! It makes sense. If a person carefully looks after a fruit tree at the very base level, they will eat its fruit. If one keeps it fed, watered, and weeded, it will bear fruit and provide something to eat and enjoy. The same goes for someone who honours their leader, boss, or fellow employees.

What do you hear from the other employees at your place of work or business? Do they speak with honour about the boss, or fellow employees? Unfortunately, all too often, you will hear only criticism, defamation of character, and accusations.

> *"If you think your boss is stupid. Remember: you wouldn't have a job if he was any smarter."*
>
> John Gotti

> *"Tend an orchard and you'll have fruit to eat. Serve the Master's interests and you'll receive honour that's sweet."*
>
> Proverbs 27:18 TPT

Perhaps honour is lacking in the workplace because we are only looking after our own interests. We have failed to see that when the company prospers, so do we. What is good for the goose is also good for the gander, if you get my meaning. If we continually criticize, condemn, or complain about our employers, we not only tear them down, but ourselves too. On the other hand, if we honour, support, and care for their interests, we will absolutely reap what we sow. It's the way of life. Treat others as you would like to be treated. Like the Golden Rule says, do unto others as you would have them do to you. In this way, you are sowing seeds for your own success. However, if you lower yourself to join the bottom of the barrel bunch, who dishonour the boss, then you will have no one to blame but yourself when things go wrong.

Please take my advice - serve those in authority with honour, and honour will be drawn to you. Live life at the workplace at a higher level by lifting up and not tearing down, and watch the honour come your way. How sweet it will taste!

THINK ON THIS... Are you serving your employer with honour or dishonour? What can you change today that will bring honour to your employer?

WEEK 11
HONOUR

Day 55

Show family affection to one another with brotherly love.
Outdo one another in showing honour.

Romans 12:10 HCSB

The word honour means to show value or high esteem to someone or something. This idea of honour is rarely seen today, while dishonour seems to be the norm. It's actually more common to see or hear dishonour. In fact, when someone is honoured, it is viewed as something weird or strange. The truth is that God calls all of us to live honourably towards other people and *"outdo one another in showing honour."* It's as if God has called us to a competition with one another.

To honour more proficiently, it is necessary to discover how we dishonour. Dishonour is shown when we are disrespectful, lack care and concern, and speak negatively about another. It can manifest in a thousand different ways, and we need to look at ourselves to see if we are honourable or not.

> *"People will forget what you said. People will forget what you did. But people will never forget how you made them feel."*
>
> Behance

Some folks believe that honour should be given only when deserved, but we are to show honour, not for any reason other than to love people as God loves them. God values people, and we are to emulate Him. Also, we give honour, not because someone deserves it, but because God commands it. For instance, I don't have to like my employer to give him/her honour. You don't have to like someone to honour them, but you do have to obey the Lord. As we honour people, our understanding of their intrinsic value will increase. The more we value others, the more we will love them. Whatever we honour, we will grow to love.

> *"For just as you judge and criticize and condemn others, (dishonour) you will be judged and criticized and condemned, and in accordance with the measure you [use to] deal out to others, it will be dealt out again to you."*
>
> Matthew 7:2 AMP (emphasis mine)

The truth is that however we choose to treat others, they will, in turn, treat us the same. Don't you think it's better to give honour to people, and in the process, they will honour you? It's better than dishonour, I can assure you!

THINK ON THIS... Today is a great day to check your honour level. If it's a little low, it's time to top it up.

WEEK 12 – DILIGENCE

Day 56

The plans of the diligent certainly lead to profit, but
anyone who is reckless certainly becomes poor.
Proverbs 21:5 HCSB

As great as a plan may be, it's the planner who is diligent in bringing it to pass that will be successful. Many people have grand ambitions, ideas, and plans, but that won't automatically lead to achievement. The realization of a great plan only happens when it is diligently followed through. Starting is easy but finishing strong is hard! Remember, it's not how you start, but how you finish that counts. Finishing is the result of diligence. A fantastic plan is only as good as the people who implement it. You could have a million-dollar plan, but it will come to zero if there is a lack of diligence.

"By failing to prepare, you are preparing to fail."
Benjamin Franklin

It takes diligence to plan. Some folks never succeed because they refuse to prepare. Planning usually precedes success. It makes sense, doesn't it? If there is no diligent planning, it's just a dream. A goal without a plan is just a wish. Wishing never wins. I wish this...I wish that. Do wishes come true? Only if the wish is put into a concrete plan of action and diligently executed. I wonder how many great ideas ended up on the drawing-room floor because no one was persistent enough to bring them to fruition.

The Lord spoke to me one evening as I was praying, and He said, *"Your preparations must exceed your expectations."*

Planning is preparation, and how much you prepare will dictate the success or failure of that plan. So many people are expecting but not planning and preparing. If you don't prepare for something, you will not see anything.

"...but anyone who is reckless certainly becomes poor." In other words, people who live life without planning will struggle to see success in their lives. Instead of planning and sticking to it, they implement it too early, and everything falls apart. Be sure to take the time to look at everything, talk to others, get good advice, and take the proper steps to ensure success.

We can have the right motivation and be eager to do something great, but we will ultimately falter without a plan. Or worse, if we don't have a plan, we have nothing to be diligent about.

Desires are fickle. They come and go. Here today, gone tomorrow! This is why it's necessary to be a diligent planner. Commitment to the plan keeps us on track. Without that diligence, we will soon lose interest in the idea.

THINK ON THIS... Do you have any plans? And, if you do, are you diligent in preparing for those plans? Remember: If you fail to plan, you are planning to fail.

WEEK 12
DILIGENCE

Day 57

The slacker craves, yet has nothing,
but the diligent is fully satisfied.
Proverbs 13:4 HCSB

Diligence means to be persistent in work or effort. A slacker, on the other hand, avoids hard work or effort. As a pastor, I can't tell you how many times I've counselled people who were struggling financially and yet weren't very diligent in pursuing a job. They desired financial security. Who doesn't? But money, from what I can see, doesn't grow on trees. They want, wish, dream, and struggle but fail to realize that it will take diligence on their part to turn the situation around. A little persistence can undoubtedly go a long way. Often, the difference between the haves and the have-nots is diligence.

"Diligence is the mother of good luck."
Benjamin Franklin

My good friend's brother is a dentist. He has many nice things and doesn't need to worry about finances, but it didn't come without a price. When he was a teenager, he worked at McDonald's after school and on weekends. When many of his friends were out goofing off or partying their lives away, he was studying. Between studying and working, he had no time to play. He was extremely diligent in his pursuit of bettering his life. Today, he has multiple dental practices and is fully satisfied. I can imagine many people said, *"McDonald's! I'm not working there - no way!"* So, instead of making money, they probably have nothing but cravings, and cravings don't pay the bills or put food on the table. Not everything we do is successful, but we can rest assured if we do our "due diligence," we will have more accomplishments than not.

THINK ON THIS... Do your 'due diligence.' It can be the difference between success or failure.

Week 12
Diligence

Day 58

Idle hands make one poor,
but diligent hands bring riches.
Proverbs 10:4 HCSB

To become poor, all you have to do is nothing. Nothing times nothing is and will always be nothing. Simple mathematics explains this concept perfectly.

When I first became a believer and heard the "prosperity" message, I sometimes thought that God would rain money down on me. Perhaps it would suddenly appear like manna, or an angel would bring it to my doorstep. Another idea was that it would come in the mail. It's not that God couldn't or wouldn't do these things, but it rarely ever happened for me. One time, I was praying for a certain amount and fully expected God to come through. Every day, I would look in the mailbox with hope and expectation and yet a week before it was needed, nothing. One day, I got a call from a friend's father who asked me if I would replace the shingles on his roof. With my lightning-fast mind, I realized after a few minutes that this could be God's provision. It wasn't at all what I wanted to do at the time. I had worked in that trade for a few years and came to dislike it immensely. My thought was, Roofing - - who in their right mind wants to do that? But, doing nothing wasn't paying off, so I did the roof and earned the money I needed.

"It is the working man who is the happy man. It is the idle man who is the miserable man."

Benjamin Franklin

The truth is that if I hadn't taken that job, I don't think I would have received the money I needed. And I learned that, *"in all labour, there is profit."* That incident changed my perspective about the value of hard work. God heard my prayer and provided. If I had been too lazy to work, I would've missed the blessing. Too many people want to become prosperous the easy way, and as attractive as that might seem, it's not the norm. The normal way is to be diligent in your work, and prosperity will soon follow.

THINK ON THIS... Are there areas in your life that are suffering because of idleness?

WEEK 12
DILIGENCE

Day 59

The diligent hand will rule,
but laziness will lead to forced labour.
Proverbs 12:24 HCSB

The Passion Translation puts it this way; *"If you want to reign in life, don't sit on your hands. Instead, work hard at doing what's right, for the slacker will end up working to make someone else succeed."*

There's something about being diligent in all that a person does that attracts success. It's entirely possible that the only difference between he who rules, and he who doesn't is diligence or the lack thereof. You don't even have to be smarter than everyone else, just more industrious.

Many people falsely believe that if they were more gifted or smarter, they could become something more. That is not the truth at all. Diligence is a better asset than brains. I have known many intelligent people who are going nowhere in life. If all it took was grey matter, they would be the ones successful and in charge, but they aren't. Why? It takes more than smarts to become successful. It takes years of hard work and diligence.

> *"Singleness of purpose is one of the chief essentials for success in life, no matter what may be one's aim."*
> John D. Rockefeller

John D. Rockefeller became one of the richest men in history. He was born the son of a con artist and, when he was sixteen, decided that school wasn't his thing and began a career, with the goal to earn $100,000.00. Did he succeed? We all know the answer. In 1902, he was worth 200 million, and before his death, he had amassed a fortune of one billion dollars.

By no means am I saying that education isn't important. It's extremely so, but it's not the only principle involved in becoming a success. There are other factors, and one of them is diligence. Many people have been successful in life, not because of anything other than diligently pursuing what they wanted to accomplish.

It's clear Rockefeller wasn't a slacker, and as a result, he became one who ruled. He became the boss, the employer, and the owner. Working for another wasn't in his DNA. He wanted more than that, and through diligence and hard work, he obtained it.

THINK ON THIS... What do you want to accomplish during your time on this Earth? What are you willing to do to accomplish those things?

WEEK 12
DILIGENCE

Day 60

Be diligent to know the state of your flocks
and look well to your herds.

Proverbs 27:23 AMP

The quickest way to ruin or failure is through neglect. To achieve and maintain success, diligence is a necessary ingredient.

> *"I went by the field of a slacker and by the vineyard of a man lacking sense. Thistles had come up everywhere, weeds covered the ground, and the stone wall was ruined. I saw, and took it to heart; I looked, and received instruction: a little sleep, a little slumber, a little folding of the arms to rest, and your poverty will come like a robber, your need, like a bandit."*
>
> Proverbs 24:30–34 HCSB

Imagine how beautiful this vineyard looked before it fell into neglect. I'm sure it was well taken care of, with no weeds or thistles and bearing good fruit. The buildings, walls, and gates would have been kept up, painted, and clean. There's no doubt that everywhere you looked, there were incredible sights to behold. This is how it is with the diligent person. They are always aware of what is going on. They keep a careful count of their herds and flocks. None are missing, and if they are, the culprit is quickly found.

Diligence takes work. Perhaps that's why some folks lack this trait and are downright lazy and neglectful. Maybe some think that things will fix themselves or the problems will magically disappear. They don't! Neglect has the power to reduce any good thing to rubble.

> *"A little neglect may breed great mischief; for want of a nail the shoe was lost; for want of the shoe the horse was lost; for want of the horse the rider was lost -- being overtaken and slain by an enemy -- all for the want of care about a horse-shoe nail."*
>
> Benjamin Franklin

THINK ON THIS... It's not how you start that counts, but how you finish. Finish well by being diligent!

WEEK 13 - IRON SHARPENS IRON

Day 61

> Iron sharpens iron, and one man sharpens another.
>
> Proverbs 27:17 HCSB

This Proverb was written during the Iron Age in the Middle East. Iron was not very pure at that time and contained other metals, such as nickel, copper, and even carbon. Pure iron is soft, and carbon steel can be as much as 1000 times harder. Iron, in those days, contained varying amounts of impurities and was of different strengths.

I once heard a man say this, *"I can tell who or what you will be like in five years, by the books your read, the music you listen to, and the people you hang with."* That sounds right to me.

When one thing sharpens another, the substance on the sharpening surface must be harder than the material being honed, such as two different alloys of iron. Similarly, one man who is strong in faith can sharpen another to help him become stronger. We may not realize it, but we have the ability to affect one another, either positively or negatively.

> *"If you want to be a sharp thinker, be around sharp people."*
>
> John Maxwell

> *"And let us consider one another in order to stir up love and good works..."*
>
> Proverbs 27:17 HCSB

We must be careful not to disassociate with everyone who challenges us. We all need people who will both encourage and challenge us to be better. We all have areas where we can improve. Years ago, I worked in various capacities at a hotel. Every six months or so, we would be called in and evaluated on our performance and attitude. When my turn came, I thought all would be well, but to my chagrin, I was challenged in an area. Well, on my way home, I was saying to myself, *"Who are they to evaluate a child of the King, a son of God, a believer? They aren't even saved!"* But wouldn't you know it, immediately the Holy Ghost spoke to me and said, *"You know Brent, they are right."* And they were. I learned two valuable lessons that day -- God can and will even use unbelievers to sharpen who we are, and a little humility can go a long way.

THINK ON THIS...

Who is sharpening you?

WEEK 13
IRON SHARPENS IRON

Day 62

As iron sharpens iron, so a man sharpens
the countenance of his friend.

Proverbs 27:17

Remember the story of Cain and Abel? Cain's countenance had fallen, but when God tried to sharpen it, he refused the help. Later, Cain killed his brother, and it negatively affected the rest of his life. I firmly believe God sends people into our lives for the sole purpose of sharpening us spiritually, mentally, and emotionally. But we must first learn to recognize them and not be offended when we feel the sharpener's grinding wheel in a particular area of our lives.

"If you keep sending every person away who challenges you, you'll never grow!"

Andy Hale

On the flip side of things, I am so thankful for the friends God has given me. They comfort, encourage, and exhort me. I can easily fall into pessimism, so I need positive people around me. There are people in my life who make me smile, keep me loved, and help me feel appreciated, and that is worth all the gold in China. You can't pay enough for those kinds of folks. They have doubly blessed me. I hope you can say the same.

We can also be the iron that sharpens the countenance of those around us, be it at work, play, church, or wherever. We are the light of the world and the salt of the earth. If we can't be happy and joyful during life's challenges, then who can?

> *"Therefore, encourage one another and build each other up as you are already doing."*
>
> 1 Thessalonians 5:11 HCSB

We are all called to encourage and build each other up. We need to look for opportunities to edify one another. Every day we should be on the lookout for someone that we can bless with our words. No matter what we're going through, there are always people facing something worse than we are.

THINK ON THIS... I challenge you to touch one person's life each day. As you encourage someone else, you will also be encouraged.

WEEK 13
IRON SHARPENS IRON

Day 63

As iron sharpens iron, so a friend sharpens a friend.
Proverbs 27:17 NLT

In the sharpening of iron with iron, both pieces change — the sharpener and the one being sharpened. This removing of the burrs refines the edge until it can easily cut through the toughest materials. In the same way one piece of iron can sharpen another one, we can influence others. We can build one another up and help each other become better people. The positive person can help the negative person. The optimist can challenge the pessimist. Good friends influence us in a positive manner.

Early on in my Christian life, I became good friends with a guy at work. When I talked to him about the Lord, he was polite and listened for a time, but after a while, he didn't want to hear any more on the subject. We continued to hang out, and over time, I found myself taking on some of his characteristics. He was negatively influencing me, and so, with great sadness, I slowly began to disassociate myself from him. If you have a friend of questionable character and find yourself becoming like them, it may be time to withdraw.

"Surround yourself with only people who are going to lift you up higher."

Oprah Winfrey

"Do not be so deceived and misled! Evil companionships (communion, associations) corrupt and deprave good manners and morals and character."

1 Corinthians 15:33 AMP

A good friend will influence you towards God, not away from Him. In the same way, bad habits and negative thoughts and actions are removed from our lives when we are sharpened by the encouragement and loving criticism of a fellow believer. Just as a blade can be polished to increase its ability to cut more cleanly, we are polished by a good friend's lifestyle and influence.

THINK ON THIS... Who are your closest friends? What type of influence are they in your life? On the flip side, what kind of friend are you?

WEEK 13
IRON SHARPENS IRON

Day 64

You use steel to sharpen steel,
and one friend sharpens another.
Proverbs 27:17 Message

A real friend is not afraid to speak the truth in love. They are the kind that will steer you in the right direction. They aren't too scared to stand up to you, if necessary, to challenge your point of view or give you an earful if that's what it takes to get your attention. But unfortunately, this kind of friend is difficult to acquire.

> *"Wounds from a sincere friend are better than many kisses from an enemy."*
>
> Proverbs 27:6 NLT

Are good friends hard to obtain? I think that if you have one genuine friend, you are fortunate. If you were to have two, that would be fantastic. If you have many, then you are beyond blessed. I can honestly say that I've been blessed with an abundance of great friends who have stuck with me for many years. Having said that, what is it that we want from a friend? What kind of friend do you want? Do you want one that tells you what you want to hear, or the type that tells you the truth, even if it stings a little? I will choose an honest friend every time.

> *"A good friend is like a four-leaf clover, hard to find and lucky to have."*
>
> Irish Proverb

A friend who won't tell you the truth is not a friend at all! A great friend isn't interested in padding your ego or justifying your wrongs; they are concerned for your well-being. They can speak the truth because they aren't in it for themselves. They care about you - the real you. So, the next time a friend challenges you a little or speaks the truth to you, don't get upset or freak out. Instead, realize what a gift you've been given. There is nothing better than a sincere friend in this life.

THINK ON THIS...

Do you get upset when a friend challenges you?

WEEK 13
IRON SHARPENS IRON

Day 65

Walk with the wise and become wise;
associate with fools and get in trouble.
Proverbs 13:20 NLT

You become like those with whom you hang around. Like attracts. Birds of a feather flock together. These are a few expressions created as a result of studying human behaviour. People usually associate with like-minded people. Sometimes this is a good thing, but it can also be a source of danger. Who you associate closely with can make or break you.

Those of us who have reared children understand this concept. We kept a close eye on who our children became companions with. If you are a parent, I would advise you to always be aware of who your children spend time with. Don't leave this to chance. They will be influenced either for good or evil. It's a rare child who knows the difference between a wise or foolish friend.

When I was young, I was the kid my friends' parents told them to avoid because I was usually in the middle of trouble, either causing it or caught up in it. I also was not a discerning person and hung out with the wrong people, which in the end, did me more harm than good. I wasn't necessarily an evil person, but for some reason, mischief followed me. Thank God, He was able to save me and deliver me from myself.

"If you hang around with chickens, you're going to cluck, and if you hang with eagles, you're going to fly."
Steve Maraboli

I have seen people use Godly characteristics in the wrong context; for example, someone who stays faithful to a friend even though they are toxic and unhealthy for them. They justify it and use faithfulness as a reason to stay connected. Yes, God wants us to be faithful, but not to people who have no desire to change. Loyalty has its place in our lives, but not to toxic people that refuse to grow. Sometimes, we need to change the people we hang around with if we want to change ourselves.

I like to surround myself with those who are smarter than me, which doesn't take much. But I know that if I do, I have a greater chance of being successful.

THINK ON THIS... This isn't easy to do, but take a friend inventory today. What do you see? Are your friends good or bad for you?

WEEK 14 - THE WICKED

Day 66

A wicked man's iniquities entrap him;
he is entangled in the ropes of his own sin.
Proverbs 5:22 HCSB

No one can escape the consequences of sin. Sin promises you more than it can deliver, takes you farther than you want to go, and costs you more than you want to pay. God gave the Ten Commandments, not as a means to handicap mankind, but to keep him free from sin's power to trap the one who indulges in it. We may think it innocent enough to sin, do or say whatever we want, and not even consider what the backlash will be. The problem is that if we don't change, eventually, there will be an adverse reaction to our sin.

"For every action, there is an equal and opposite reaction."

John Newton

Sin also creates a greater problem than just the act itself. When a person sins, invisible cords, like ropes, begin to entangle their hearts and mind. They ensnare the person until they are completely bound by them. Just last week, I saw this play out before my eyes in a very real and scary manner. I was waiting in my car for the light to change when I saw a young man walking by. He was yelling, screaming, and waving his arms uncontrollably. Undoubtedly, he was under the influence of some form of drug. He likely never anticipated things would escalate to this level when he first tried drugs. How about the alcoholic who must drink every day and cannot stop, for his cravings are severe. The same goes for the pornography addict, who mistakenly thought that viewing it was as harmless as the porn pushers intended it to be. Before he realized, it had wrapped powerful, invisible ropes around his heart and mind, and it was all he could think about. Guilt and shame are its lasting effects.

The good news is that Jesus is the power that can set the sinner free, and millions of people can testify of that in their lives. I was bound by sin, but now, I am free by the divine influence of God in my life. You may be held in bondage to sin's power right now but know this - if you turn to God in faith, He will set you free, both from the sin itself and from its heinous consequences in your life.

THINK ON THIS…Is there an area in your life where you feel bound up with invisible cords? Turn to God in faith, and let Him break those cords.

WEEK 14
THE WICKED

Day 67

The tongue of the righteous is pure silver;
the heart of the wicked is of little value.
Proverbs 10:20 HCSB

From the abundance of the heart, the mouth speaks. A righteous heart should put forth righteous speech. Whatever is in the heart will eventually make its way out of the mouth. If the heart is filled with good things, like the Word of God, then that will be what comes out. Conversely, a person who continuously fills their heart with evil things will have a wicked mouth.

Before I was born again, my mouth would never have been considered valuable as pure silver. On the contrary, it was perverse, full of evil and cursing. When Jesus came into my heart, a remarkable transformation occurred - my mouth began to change. I used to swear constantly, and four-letter words were the bulk of my speech. They were my adjectives, adverbs, and exclamations. I used cuss words to describe everything in life, and it was normal for me. I didn't know any better. I distinctly remember trying to swear the day after I was saved. I used the name of the Lord in vain, and it was awful. I cursed, and it felt horribly wrong. It simply didn't sound or feel right anymore. I couldn't say those words anymore.

> *"No foul language is to come from your mouth, but only what is good for building up someone in need, so that it gives grace to those who hear."*

Apostle Paul
Ephesians 4:29 HCSB

Our words have the power to help or hinder, heal, or cut, and bless rather than curse. If our words cannot be described as pure silver, then perhaps we need to wash our mouth out with soap like mom used to do, only in a spiritual sense. God intended our tongues to be a source of life, strength, and goodness, not evil. I encourage you today to take inventory of your words and measure them against the Word of God. Are they pure silver, or are they tainted in some manner?

THINK ON THIS... Does your speech produce value in other people's lives?

Week 14
The Wicked

Day 68

The righteous will never be shaken,
but the wicked will not remain on the earth.
Proverbs 10:30 HCSB

Good people last—they can't be moved;
the wicked are here today, gone tomorrow.
Proverbs 10:30 Message

The book of Proverbs contrasts the righteous with the wicked. Righteous refers to those who, by the grace of God, have accepted salvation by faith in Jesus' death and resurrection. The wicked are those who have not. Both live on the earth, but they are living two totally different lives. The righteous have God on their side; the wicked do not. Without Christ, the wicked will eventually perish from the earth. The righteous, on the other hand, will always be safe and secure in the Lord. He cannot be moved, and anyone who is in Christ will echo this sentiment.

It doesn't matter what happens in life; a believer in Christ has what others do not – long-term security. The Lord has promised to *"never leave or forsake"* those who are His. We don't know what will happen in our lifetime, whether good or evil. We can't predict what will occur in our lives, peace, or trouble. We cannot control these things, but we can live in security because we have God in our lives.

"Trust in the Lord and do what is good; dwell in the land and live securely."

Psalm 37:3 HCSB

We will not be moved - not by circumstances, fear, or anything else that comes against us. If God is anything, it is this - He is God, and He can't be defeated! He is our victory in everything! If we trust in Him and not in what we can see or understand, He will always bring us through the fire and the flood. Nothing is too difficult for God, and therefore, nothing is too hard for Him in our lives.

> *"We are secure, not because we hold tightly to Jesus, but because He holds tightly to us."*
>
> R.C. Sproul

You can have faith in God no matter what the circumstances of life throw at you. God is not up there wringing His hands and worrying about your life. No, He has it all under control. The God who created the earth, the stars, the moon, and all that we see, is great enough to keep you secure and safe. We don't have to be moved or shaken by what others feel or see. God is bigger than all that! Let God be big in your life!

THINK ON THIS... Is God the stronghold in your life? Do not let what you see dictate your feelings of security and safety.

Week 14
The Wicked

Day 69

The Lord is far from the wicked,
but He hears the prayer of the righteous.
Proverbs 15:29 HCSB

I love this verse. It is one of my "go-to" scriptures when I spend time with the Lord. It gives me faith that God is listening to me when I speak to Him. God is not deaf. He hears us, even when we don't think He does. In fact, let me say this, God has heard every prayer you have spoken, even the ones you've forgotten. There have been times in my life when I thought prayers, I had said years ago were never going to materialize, and then one day, there it was. God never forgot what we talked about, even when I did. He never gave up on my prayers, even when I had. Listen - a tear doesn't drop, and a hair doesn't fall to the ground that He isn't aware of. God never forgets our prayers.

> *"Indeed, the Lord's hand is not too short to save, and His ear is not too deaf to hear."*
>
> Isaiah 59:1 HCSB

This is obviously where faith comes into play. When you pray, do you believe God has heard you? Of course, our prayers can't be out of His will. He still hears but is not obligated to answer. If we pray according to His will, we know that He hears us. Therefore, our prayers must never be self-motivated or selfish. Otherwise, it may appear to many that God has indeed lost His hearing.

God even knows what we pray about before we speak a word. He knows what is in our hearts. Sometimes He even answers before we say anything. That's how awesome and omniscient He is. Nothing escapes His gaze.

> *"God answers prayer, He just doesn't always answer them your way."*
>
> Lou Holtz

I believe that if there is a lack of prayer in the church world, it's because people don't think God hears them. Because if we really and truly believed God hears us when we pray, we would never stop praying. It's sad, but I seriously think people struggle to pray because they don't believe He hears them. Let me assure you - God hears you when you pray!

This doesn't mean everything you've ever talked about will happen just as you want it to. The truth is that while God hears all our prayers, He answers them in accordance with His own will. The Holy Spirit intercedes on behalf of all the saints according to the will of God. This means that, yes, God hears us when we pray, but He works to bring those answers to us in line with His will. He decided this ages ago and cannot do anything to the contrary. The good news is that God's will has been and always will be for our highest good. We may pray improperly at times, but I believe God works everything out for our good in the end.

THINK ON THIS... Prayer does us no good unless we pray. Spend some quality time with Him today because He hears you.

Week 14
The Wicked

Day 70

No disaster overcomes the righteous,
but the wicked are full of misery.
Proverbs 12:21 HCSB

Both the wicked and the righteous will face horrible things at some point in their lives. Troubles come to us all; no one is exempt. But even in disaster, God promises that His people will overcome. The same cannot be said of the wicked. God is a very present help in times of trouble, but sadly for those who don't know the Lord, this is not the case. They must go through life's problems and struggles in their own strength, with no one to help them. How terrible it must be to contract a disease or see a family member succumb to cancer or the like and have no one to trust in except what doctors and medicine can offer? What is their end - only misery, pain, and suffering, with no relief in sight? My heart goes out to anyone who doesn't have the Lord to help them in their suffering.

The good news for the believer is that although suffering may still come into their lives, they have an anchor of the soul that the unbeliever doesn't have. God is our hope and very present help in times of difficulty and disaster. He guarantees to be with us in difficulty and will never, ever leave us. He assures us peace amid the storm. He promises to keep our head above the floods and to take us through the fires of tribulation and troubles. He is our refuge when we have nowhere to turn.

"Hard times only reveal our true friends."

Unknown

Not only that, but He has promised to give us joy in every trial and circumstance if we choose to accept it. We can rejoice, knowing that God is with us and has promised to take us through to the other side. He is with us even when it may not feel like it. He is omnipresent. He sees it all, and He is for you. Never forget that in every trial and affliction you face, He is your best friend, your greatest ally, and your greatest source of strength. Trust in Him, and He will never let you down.

No matter how bad it might look today, tomorrow is another day, and circumstances are always subject to change. Today, I can't remember the challenges of yesteryear, but I know they happened. With God, there is no disaster so devastating that He cannot help us through.

THINK ON THIS... Are you facing a challenge right now? If you are, don't forget to trust in the Lord!

WEEK 15 – CONTENTION

Day 71

A hot-tempered man stirs up strife,
but he who is slow to anger appeases contention.
Proverbs 15:18 AMP

Temper, temper, temper! I remember many times in school during gym class that contentions and disputes would arise, inevitably tempers would flare, and fights would occur. Hot-headed, competitive guys who had to win at any cost didn't realize that they would pay the price for their unruliness. If not now, then later in life.

The definition of *"to lose your temper"* is this - you become so angry that you shout at someone or demonstrate in some other way that you are no longer in control of yourself. When a person loses their temper, nothing good ever comes of it.

Why do people lose their temper? Were they born this way? Are some people better at keeping their cool than others? I believe that losing one's temper is a learned behaviour, probably starting at a very young age and never curbed. Often, this can be observed in the grocery store, as a youngster will begin screaming, crying, and making a scene, much to the chagrin of both parent and spectator. Sometimes, I will move closer and examine the situation further. It amazes me how often the parents seem to be clueless about how to handle it. What's worse is parents who think this behaviour is funny and encourage it. Unfortunately, they have no idea what they are empowering, do they?

The problem with this is that the hot-tempered person will live a life that is always full of contention. Losing one's temper gets easier the more it's unleashed. It doesn't take much for these people to "fly off the handle." While they may believe that "losing it" will win the day, they are highly mistaken. When contention arises, no one wins!

> *"The best remedy for a short temper is a long walk."*
>
> Robert Joubert

> *"My dearly loved brothers, understand this: Everyone must be quick to hear, slow to speak, and slow to anger, for man's anger does not accomplish God's righteousness."*
>
> James 1:19–20 HCSB

What's the antidote for a quick temper? First, realize that anger never accomplishes the will of God in our lives. Second, choose to become a person who isn't easily angered. When tempted to blow your top, stop, take a deep breath, and walk away. Take control of your temper, and you will ultimately take control of your life.

THINK ON THIS... Have you allowed yourself to be a 'hothead,' or are you 'cool as a cucumber' when contentions arise? The next time you find yourself in a place of contention, take a long walk.

WEEK 15
CONTENTION

Day 72

The beginning of strife is like releasing water; therefore, stop contention before a quarrel starts.

Proverbs 17:14

Too often, contention results from people fighting for their rights or their own way. It starts out harmlessly enough but can turn ugly very quickly. Stopping it before it gains momentum is the sure-fire way to end it. The writer of Proverbs likens this to the releasing of water. I don't know the context, but we get the gist of it. Water is easily controlled when it's not allowed to increase in pressure and volume, so it is with contention. However, suppose water is not controlled when it is a trickle. In that case, it will eventually push through the barriers and grow stronger until it's pouring out of control and causing destruction.

> *"And there was quarrelling between the herdsmen of Abram's livestock and the herdsmen of Lot's livestock. At that time the Canaanites and the Perizzites were living in the land. Then Abram said to Lot, "Please, let's not have quarrelling between you and me, or between your herdsmen and my herdsmen, since we are relatives. Isn't the whole land before you? Separate from me: if you go to the left, I will go to the right; if you go to the right, I will go to the left.""*
>
> Genesis 13:7–9 HCSB

Here is an excellent account of how to deal with contention. The herdsmen of Abram and Lot were disputing over grazing space and water rights - important things for sure. As important as they were, Abram wasn't going to let it cause strife and division with his relative. He did the mature thing and backed down. Instead of fighting for his rights, he gave them up and offered Lot his pick of the land. His attitude was, if you want this, it's yours. If not, then go the other way. It doesn't matter to me because either way, we both win. I like Abram's thinking. He was able to curb the contention before things got out of hand.

> *"Your opponent's wrong doesn't automatically make you right. Most fights aren't about who's right; they are contentions over degrees of wrongness."*
>
> Richelle E. Goodrich,
> *Making Wishes*

Many hurt feelings would be avoided in our relationships if we stop the disagreements early on. Marriages would be better, relationships stronger, and our lives more peaceful if we would simply stop contention before it gains momentum.

THINK ON THIS... You don't have to be right all the time. To avoid contention and strife, it's often better to give in than to fight for your rights.

Week 15
Contention

Day 73

A brother offended is harder to win than a strong city,
and contentions are like the bars of a castle.

Proverbs 18:19

People who wish to be offended will always find some
occasion for taking offence.

John Wesley

Offence - is there anything worse? I don't know, at least not where relationships are concerned there isn't. Jesus said that offences would come to all of us in life - no one is exempt. Let's face it, you will be offended at some point, but the issue isn't the offence itself, but rather, what you do about it. I've lost friends over issues that I can't, for the life of me, remember what they were, and probably, so have you. We may believe ourselves to be in the right about it, but the truth is, if the friendship is ruined, then we have all lost. You know, the worst thing about it is that it's almost impossible to restore the relationship.

The writer says it's easier to take a strong city by force than win the offended back to relationship. Yikes! Why? Because the contention between the two parties has become prison bars of their own making. Offences create invisible bars of iron in the hearts of people, and if mishandled, will never be released, keeping them in a spiritual prison of sorts for the rest of their lives.

"Individuals who deliberately decide not to take offence, lead happier, more productive lives."

Lloyd D. Newell

The way steel bars of the gates of a castle prevent everyone from going in and out, so the offence created by contention keeps people apart, unable to connect in relationship again. While we may believe contentions are harmless, they are anything but. We may innocently believe that the only person harmed is the one who is mistaken, but that's incorrect; everyone is affected to some degree or another.

THINK ON THIS... Does being right matter so much that we would risk losing a friend over it? Wouldn't it be more prudent to give up before it gets to that point?

Week 15
Contention

Day 74

For lack of wood the fire goes out, and where there is no whisperer, contention ceases.

Proverbs 26:20 AMP

Like Smokey the Bear says, *"Only you can prevent forest fires."* Other than lightning strikes, most fires are caused by careless people – a cigarette flicked out the car window, campfires left smouldering, or a carelessly tossed match. Just as a fire can be prevented, so can contention, which, if given enough fuel, will continue to grow in scope and scale.

> *"Quarrel not at all. No man resolved to make the most of himself can spare time for personal contention. Better to give your path to the dog than be bitten by him."*
>
> Abraham Lincoln

As James 3:5 states, *"Consider how large a forest a small fire ignites."* Even so, all it takes is a whisper to stir up the embers of contention and cause it to grow. How often in a marriage do we see this happen? An argument breaks out, and just when it starts to fizzle, someone whispers something, and wind blows on the fire again. Instead of losing its force and dying out, the contention burns brighter. Feelings are hurt, painful memories are created, and walls are built - all because of a whisper.

If you want to put a fire out, it makes perfect sense to stop giving it wood to burn. Same with contention. It can't be halted until someone stops it. It takes two to fight, and if one stops, the fight stops.

THINK ON THIS... Next time you're tempted to add fuel to the fire, keep it to yourself. The life you save may be your own!

WEEK 15
CONTENTION

Day 75

Only by pride cometh contention:
But with the well advised is wisdom.
Proverbs 13:10 KJV

Pride has many faces and facets, one of which is contention. It reveals itself in life every day, whether at home, the office, playground, sports arena, or in relationships. People think they are righteously quarrelling over being right, but the truth is that they are fighting over pride.

Why do we feel this "need" to be right all the time? I believe it all started in the garden with Adam and Eve, who, after falling into sin, tried to cover it up. When God asked each of them about it, they were quick to blame someone else. Adam blamed the woman God gave him, and the woman deferred to the serpent. As a result of this unfortunate incident, humanity has struggled to develop a proper and godly sense of righteousness. Instead of understanding and receiving the rightness that comes from God alone, many unknowingly strive to find it in being right. There seems to be a deep-seated need in people to feel "right." I understand this. However, the problem here is that this need to be right becomes the driving force that reveals one face of pride called contention. As we fight for our rights, pride sticks its ugly face out, and the result is contention.

> *"Another face of pride is contention. Arguments, fights, unrighteous dominions, generation gaps, divorces, spouse abuse, riots and disturbances, all fall into the category of pride."*

Ezra Taft Benson

"Arrogant know-it-alls stir up discord, but wise men and women listen to each other's counsel."
Proverbs 13:10 Message

Perhaps we have this sense of rightness in us because it makes us feel better about ourselves. After all, who wants to be wrong? People desire to be wise. It was one of the reasons Eve partook of the forbidden fruit. The desire to be wise and intelligent is still around, and it's the cause of many a contention.

I've studied marriage for many years. One thing I've noticed is that when one person says something, the other immediately corrects them. It might be as innocent as a wrong time, date, or some other measure, but it quickly becomes a point of contention. *"No, it was 7:10, not 7:15, it was fifty bucks, not forty,"* and so on. The arguments ensue as they fight to be right. My wife and I decided long ago that these mundane topics are not worth fighting about. As a result, our marriage has become much more peaceful and happier. Many marriages have ended in divorce over the issue of being right. Why jeopardize the relationship with the love of your life over being right? Instead, why don't we concede the point and move on? It's only our pride on the line, after all. Don't be too proud to let things go!

THINK ON THIS... Do you struggle to let others be right? If your opinion is challenged, how does it affect you? Can you hear wisdom from others, or do you absolutely have to be right?

WEEK 16 – KNOWLEDGE

Day 76

A wise warrior is better than a strong one,
and a man of knowledge than one of strength.
Proverbs 24:5 HCSB

Brute force or wisdom, which is better? Hulk, smash, can be handy for some things but not everything. Certain things need to be handled with wisdom; thus, some fights cannot be won by strength alone. Put the two together, and you have an unbeatable duo. Also, knowledge can be more beneficial than strength, and the understanding of how to get it done can do much more than brute force will. It takes good old-fashioned know-how to get the job done. Here is a great story to illustrate this principle.

A giant ship's engine failed, and the owners tried one expert after another, but none of them could figure but how to fix the problem. Then they brought in an older man who had been repairing ships since he was young. He carried a large bag of tools with him, and when he arrived, immediately went to work. He inspected the engine very carefully from top to bottom.

Two of the ship's owners were there, watching the man, hoping he would know what to do. After looking things over, the repairman reached into his bag, pulled out a small hammer and gently tapped something. Instantly, the engine lurched into life. It was fixed. Just like that, the problem was solved.

A week later, the owners received a bill for $10,000 from the elderly man. *"What?"* the owners exclaimed. *"He hardly did anything!"*

So, they wrote him a note saying, *"Please send us an itemized bill."* This is what they received in response.

Tapping with a hammer...................... $2.00
Knowing where to tap......................... $9,998.00

Effort is important, but knowing where to make the effort makes all the difference!

This is what wisdom and knowledge have going for them. The *where*, the *how*, and the *when* to do something is far more useful than strength alone. What's the point of the force of a hammer if you have no idea what or where to hit? In this situation, power is pointless.

"Wisdom is always an overmatch for strength."
Phil Jackson

THINK ON THIS... Work smarter, not harder, is the wisdom handed down through the ages. The good news is that if you ask God for wisdom, He is more than willing to give it.

WEEK 16

KNOWLEDGE

Day 77

If you stop listening to correction, my son,
you will stray from the words of knowledge.

Proverbs 19:27 HCSB

Throughout the book of Proverbs, knowledge is a significant theme in living a successful life. Without knowledge, there's a higher probability of mistakes and failures. One key to overcoming is to listen to the wisdom of correction, which is not something most of us enjoy. The way to knowledge is to listen to those who have it.

I like working on cars, doing the mechanics, and fixing them up, but sometimes my knowledge is limited. I jokingly call myself the "King of Twice" because I will do something only to find out that I didn't quite get it right or that there was a better way. The truth is that there are people who have the knowledge we need in life, and if we ignore, stop asking, or refuse to listen when they speak, failure is not far behind. I have a great friend, who has been rebuilding cars for many years, and I have the privilege to listen and watch him work on cars. He has saved me time and money because of the great knowledge and experience he has accrued. But, and I will say it again, but one must listen to learn. If we stop listening to others, we will stray from the knowledge we desperately need to learn, grow, and ultimately succeed.

"Knowing what you don't know is more useful than being brilliant."

Charlie Mungor

"Because wisdom is protection as money is protection, and the advantage of knowledge is that wisdom preserves the life of its owner."

Ecclesiastes 7:12 HCSB

When I became a Christian many years ago, I was delivered from sin and have since learned that staying away from it produces a very happy life. Sin ruins our life, but the knowledge of God enhances it. We may think that God doesn't want us to sin because He wants to steal our fun or is a dictator, but the truth is, sin destroys us. It's one reason our Heavenly Father sent His Son Jesus into the world - to free us from the grasp and consequences of sin. Many people are ignorant of this fact. The Word of God clearly teaches and urges us to flee from sin so that we can have a great life. We don't have to learn this the hard way, but if we read and listen to what God says in His Word, we can have all the knowledge we need to escape the perils of sin.

THINK ON THIS...

When people talk to you, do you really listen?

WEEK 16
KNOWLEDGE

Day 78

For teaching shrewdness to the inexperienced,
knowledge and discretion to a young man…

Proverbs 1:4 HCSB

The remarkable thing about the Word of God is that it can give people wisdom, knowledge, discretion, and the power to become more mature than what you are at your present age.

There is no fool like an old fool - someone who refuses to learn. The Word of God is the great equalizer! I've observed both foolish older folks and wise younger ones. What was the difference? One didn't learn the knowledge of God, while the other held fast to it. The knowledge of God is the most valuable thing we can acquire. It offers us the power to make wise decisions in every area of life. To anyone who will listen, God gives the ability to attain experience and wisdom without going through the School of Hard Knocks. God gave us His Word to keep us informed about life so that we don't have to go through rough times to gain experience. For instance, we don't have to burn our hands on a stove to understand that eventually, it gets too hot for us to handle, do we? The same thing with the Word of God - it gives us knowledge about what we should or shouldn't do. We don't have to go through life stumbling day in and day out trying to gain wisdom and understanding because God has provided it in His Word.

"Knowing what you don't know is more useful than being brilliant."

Charlie Mungor

"Because wisdom is protection as money is protection, and the advantage of knowledge is that wisdom preserves the life of its owner."

Ecclesiastes 7:12 HCSB

When I became a Christian many years ago, I was delivered from sin and have since learned that staying away from it produces a very happy life. Sin ruins our life, but the knowledge of God enhances it. We may think that God doesn't want us to sin because He wants to steal our fun or is a dictator, but the truth is, sin destroys us. It's one reason our Heavenly Father sent His Son Jesus into the world - to free us from the grasp and consequences of sin. Many people are ignorant of this fact. The Word of God clearly teaches and urges us to flee from sin so that we can have a great life. We don't have to learn this the hard way, but if we read and listen to what God says in His Word, we can have all the knowledge we need to escape the perils of sin.

THINK ON THIS... Are you listening to knowledge or still learning the hard way?

WEEK 16
KNOWLEDGE

Day 79

Listen closely, pay attention to the words of the wise,
and apply your mind to my knowledge.
Proverbs 22:17 HCSB

Knowledge is great, but if we don't use it and apply it to our lives, it is useless to us. Knowledge is supreme, but only if we make use of it. The Bible is chock full of the wonderful, life-changing knowledge of God. Yet, if it sits collecting dust on the coffee table, unopened on the app on your phone, or lying dormant on the back seat of your car, it's inconsequential; without the ability to help you.

As a young man, new in the faith, I struggled with what is known as "sin consciousness," meaning I spent way too much time thinking about what a rotten sinner I was and not enough on the fact that God had forgiven me. This caused me to feel condemned and bad about myself - not God's plan at all. My Bible College Director encouraged me to write out scripture on 3x5 recipe cards and read them throughout the day. So that's what I did. I chose 2 Corinthians 5:21, which says, *"He made the One who knew no sin be sin for us, so that we might become the righteousness of God in Christ."* I meditated on that verse night after night as I delivered newspapers, and suddenly, it was as if it dropped straight from my head into my heart. Immediately, I was changed! I truly began to feel like the righteousness of God, no longer plagued by a sin consciousness. But it didn't happen without some mental application on my part. The knowledge was there all along, but if it's not used, it can't do anything. We must read, meditate, and speak the Word of God for its knowledge to help and change us.

> *"Wrote my way out of the hood...thought my way out of poverty! Don't tell me that knowledge isn't power. Education changes everything."*
>
> Brandi L. Bates

Knowledge gives power, and God's knowledge trumps all of it, for its power helps us, not only in this life but also the next. God has given us all the knowledge we will ever need in a book called, The Bible. It's the most powerful book in the universe, but it won't benefit us unless we read and do what it tells us.

THINK ON THIS... Are you growing in the knowledge of God? Do you spend time in His Word? Take time everyday to read and meditate on Scripture, and the benefits will soon reveal themselves.

WEEK 16
KNOWLEDGE

Day 80

Even zeal is not good without knowledge,
and the one who acts hastily sins.
Proverbs 19:2 HCSB

Have you ever bought something only to regret it later, acted before you thought, or spoke before you should have? Sometimes we let our zeal blind us to what knowledge would have revealed. We buy something before taking the time to investigate it because it's a great deal. I have a friend who used to say this, *"Another bus comes every 15 minutes,"* meaning good deals are always there, and they will come to the one who waits.

Fools jump in where angels fear to tread is a wise, old saying. Too often, we are guilty of this at some point in our lives. That's why the Bible encourages us to *"ponder the paths of our feet."* We seem to fear losing out on a good deal, and it's this fear that causes our misfortune. I know people who were conned out of a great deal of money because of the *"too good to be true"* opportunity. The reality is, if it seems too good to be true, then it probably is. It is best to walk away and study it a little more closely. Upon greater scrutiny, you will probably recognize the cleverly hidden snare.

> *"Get-rich-quick thinking leads to three basic errors:*
>
> *(1) Getting involved with things you cannot understand.*
>
> *(2) Risking funds you cannot afford to lose, that is, borrowed funds; and*

> *(3) Making hasty decisions. Each of these actions violates one or more biblical principles... Together they constitute a sin called greed."*
>
> Larry Burkett

Can we act too hastily, move too fast, or jump without thinking things through? For sure, and it almost always brings regret. What in the world was I thinking? Why did I do that? Why didn't someone tell me? Oh, they probably did, but you weren't listening. Are there times when a quick move is beneficial? Yes, but even then, take the time to make sure it's what you really want and that it won't eventually cost you more than you wanted to pay. Take the time to gain the knowledge needed to make good and godly decisions in life. I guarantee it will never be a waste of time.

THINK ON THIS... Do you remember a time when you made a hasty decision and it cost you? Take the time to ponder the paths your feet take. Be a little more patient, and you will be rewarded.

WEEK 17 - WORRY & ANXIETY

Day 81

Anxiety in a man's heart weighs it down,
but a good word cheers it up.
Proverbs 12:25 HCSB

The *Oxford Dictionary* defines anxiety as *"A feeling of worry, nervousness, or unease, typically about an imminent event or something with an uncertain outcome."*

Do you struggle with anxiety and worry? Are the cares of this life taking over your emotional state from day to day? Do you fret about things? Do you find yourself becoming fearful or scared of what may happen in your life? I have found that most things we fear never come to pass. Anxiety is another form of fear, and we need to tell it to leave us, for it must not have a place in our hearts and minds. God hasn't called us to be anxiety-driven people, but people of peace and happiness.

Anxiety is never a good thing. We need to learn how to overcome its powerful, adverse effects in our lives. Everyone who has ever lived on planet earth has experienced anxiety at some point or another. No one is exempt. But do we have to allow it to have its way, bringing us down, keeping us up all night, and generally disrupting our lives? No, I don't believe so.

> *"Men's hearts failing them from fear and the expectation of those things which are coming on the earth, for the powers of the heavens will be shaken."*
>
> Luke 21:26

In plain English, worry and anxiety are usually caused by a fearful expectation of what life will bring. For some, worry is a state of being. It's not necessarily a real thing, but a thing contrived in the heart and mind. Anxiety literally weighs a person down. It would be like having weights tied to your body that you must drag around every single day. Anxiety can produce discouragement and depression. If left unchecked, it can become a stronghold and negatively affect our disposition.

> *"When I look back on all these worries, I remember the story of the old man who said on his deathbed that he had had a lot of trouble in his life, most of which had never happened."*
>
> Winston Churchill

On the flip side of things, a good word cheers the heart and overcomes anxiety and worry. With all the negative news and the uncertainty of life we are inundated with daily, it's easy to become affected by it. But all it takes to overcome it is a good word. I'm so thankful for the Word of God that we can stand on to help us in times of trouble. Thank God for family and friends that have spoken good things into our lives and broken the power of anxiety. There's enough junk being spewed out every day by doomsayers and negative people that a good word spoken can be very beneficial.

THINK ON THIS... Don't worry about what you can't control. Why concern yourself with what you cannot change?

WEEK 17
WORRY & ANXIETY

Day 82

All the days of the desponding and afflicted are made
evil [by anxious thoughts and forebodings],
but he who has a glad heart has a continual feast
[regardless of circumstances].

Proverbs 15:15 AMP

Anxious thoughts? Forebodings? Sometimes people start believing that something terrible is about to happen to them, but let me assure you, that is probably not the case. Life certainly has its fair share of difficulties, but why worry about what hasn't happened? It makes no sense to do so. Anxiety can make life seem far worse than it really is. Worry can afflict us with mental strain, fear, insecurities, and even physical problems. From what we have learned, many of the illnesses people are diagnosed with have their origins in worry, anxiety, and stress.

It all comes down to either the condition of the heart or mind, as both are affected by anxiety and worry. It's incredible how the things a person thinks about can affect the depth of their happiness. We are happy or not, based solely upon what we think about. This is why we are instructed in the book of Philippians to think about what is good, virtuous, beautiful, honourable, pure, holy, etc. The level of life we experience has a lot to do with how we think. If you think that life is bad or rough, then it is. If you think life is good, then it is.

"Do not anticipate trouble or worry about what may never happen. Keep in the sunlight."

Benjamin Franklin

He who has a glad heart doesn't experience these negative things. That's why we are encouraged by the Apostle Paul to rejoice, and then again, rejoice some more. Paul, who wrote Philippians while tied to a guard in jail, had every reason to be anxious. Rather than fret and worry about his situation, he wrote this book instructing people to rejoice and be glad regardless of their circumstances. How was Paul able to remain joyful in such a horrible situation? It was because he knew that the God He served was bigger than any problem that came his way, real or imagined.

God is bigger and stronger than any problems we face here on earth, and He has promised to be with us through them all. Trust in God, and He will give you a reason to be happy.

THINK ON THIS... Where have your thoughts taken you recently? Are they full of hope and light, or depression and foreboding? You have the choice each day to think about the right things.

WEEK 17
WORRY & ANXIETY

Day 83

So do not worry or be anxious about tomorrow, for
tomorrow will have worries and anxieties of its own.
Sufficient for each day is its own trouble.

Matthew 6:34 AMP

Let's face it, most of our worries are simply caring about what will or won't happen tomorrow. We like to think ahead, but it usually brings about more trouble than what it is worth. I love what Jesus told us here in this verse. First, He said, *"Don't worry about tomorrow."* Let's think about this for a second. What does He mean when He says don't? Don't is don't. It means, do not. I think if we did this, we would all be a much happier bunch. Why shouldn't we worry about tomorrow? Because Jesus said that there is enough to worry about today. In other words, why add tomorrow's anxieties to today's? Why spend time thinking about what isn't here yet? His instruction to us is to live each day as it comes so that we can put things into their proper perspective. Remember – you cannot always control what happens to you, but you can control what happens in you.

> *"If you want to conquer the anxiety of life, live in the moment, live in the breath."*
>
> Amit Ray

Jesus ended this subject by saying, *"Sufficient for each day is its own trouble."* If we start worrying about tomorrow, we add weights that we were never designed to carry. Each day that we live here on planet earth will give us all we can handle. We certainly don't need to add to it unnecessarily. While we may believe worrying somehow adds to our lives, it actually subtracts from us. Anxiety and worry steal our joy, strength, and the very life of God. We can be happy if we concentrate on what needs to be looked after for today. Anytime we add to this list from the future, we will needlessly weigh ourselves down. Take the Master's advice and *"Don't!"*

"It ain't no use putting up your umbrella till it rains!"
Alice Caldwell Rice

THINK ON THIS... Are you a worrywart? Do you spend time and effort being anxious about tomorrow? Don't waste anymore time doing that; take care of today, and tomorrow will take care of itself.

WEEK 17
WORRY & ANXIETY

Day 84

Casting the whole of your care [all your anxieties,
all your worries, all your concerns, once and for all]
on Him, for He cares for you affectionately
and cares about you watchfully.

I Peter 5:7 AMP

Jesus once warned His listeners to avoid the *"cares of this life,"* as they were able to steal the Word of God from their hearts and cause it to become unfruitful. You can't care about too many things because whatever you care about grows to become the most potent force in your heart. Can we have too many cares? Yes, we can. As believers, we are instructed to *"Trust in the Lord with all of our heart."* How can we do so if we are carrying the weight of the world on our shoulders? This verse tells us to cast our cares on the Lord because He is bigger and can carry more weight than we can. But to do that, we must do the casting. It's kind of like sitting in a boat and trying to catch fish without taking your rod and reel and casting into the water. If we never cast, we can't catch a fish. If we never cast our burdens on the Lord, He can't take them.

Do you believe that God cares for you? He does with great affection, and He watches over you, but He needs your cooperation.

"Every tomorrow has two handles. We can take hold of it with the handle of anxiety or the handle of faith."

Henry Ward Beecher

We are to take all our anxieties, cares, worries, and concerns, and give them to Jesus. We must make a concerted effort to do this. Typically, we assume this is happening, but often it isn't. God does His part when we do ours. All He requires of us is the casting. To do that, we must be willing to let go of what we are currently carrying. I know this is hard for some folks because they like worrying. I remember commenting to someone one time that I don't fret about the current gas prices, I just buy it, and that's that. Regardless of what the price is - if I need it, I buy it. My worrying will not change a thing, so I don't let it concern me. This person replied, *"You don't worry about this stuff? Don't you care?"* Of course, I do, but that doesn't give me the right to carry it. To care doesn't mean we have to worry or be anxious about a thing. If I worry about something, it doesn't prove that I am more concerned about it. Worry is not a good demonstration of caring, although many think it is. A better way to deal with worry would be to give it to God and then trust Him to carry it for you as He promised He would.

THINK ON THIS... Are you casting all your cares upon Him? He cares for you, and wants you to stop carrying those burdens. Let Him have them today.

Week 17
Worry & Anxiety

Day 85

Don't worry about anything, but in everything,
through prayer and petition with thanksgiving,
let your requests be made known to God.
And the peace of God, which surpasses every thought,
will guard your hearts and minds in Christ Jesus.
Philippians 4:6–7 HCSB

This verse may be the one we love the most but obey the least. Ouch! We love the idea that God hears our requests and guards our hearts, but what we miss is the prerequisite for it, which is, *"Don't worry about anything."* It's the first point, not the second or third. The command here is not to worry about anything, nada, zip, nothing, no thing at all. We need to make a commitment not to worry.

I remember when I would be sitting and worrying about stuff, and Barb would ask me what I was doing. I replied, *"Thinking."* She would respond with, *"No, you're worrying."* And you know what, she was usually, not always, but usually correct. Worry leads to a lack of peace in our lives. God sent Jesus, the Prince of Peace, to give us peace. We must do our very best to allow that peace to work in our lives.

How do we do this? By prayer and petitions, with thanksgiving, we come to God with our requests. To stop worrying, we must talk to God. If we don't, we can't overcome it. We can't simply muster up the willpower to combat worry. That won't work. We need help, and God is a very present help in times of trouble.

We can expect answers when we make a stand to not worry and spend quality time with God. And that's when His peace comes in. I know the Bible also says that God knows what we want before we ask, but this doesn't mean we shouldn't ask.

I love this verse. It is telling us to spend time with God. Then, and only then, will we have the peace that overcomes all worry and guards our hearts and minds. How does it guard? When we spend time with Him, it produces faith in us that God is in control. Without prayer, worry is still in control and continues to affect our hearts and minds.

After time is spent with the Lord in prayer, He releases the peace that only He can give, the kind that surpasses every worried and anxious thought. It becomes a garrison around our hearts and minds and will protect us. Within that peace, we win the battle over worry, anxiety, and fear. The problem is that most people don't follow the advice given in these passages of Scripture. The hardest part is letting go of our worries.

> *"Anxiety does not empty tomorrow of its sorrows, but only empties today of its strength."*
>
> Charles Spurgeon

THINK ON THIS...

Be intentional to overcome the power of worry in your life.

WEEK 18 - WISE COUNSEL

Day 86

> A fool's way is right in his own eyes,
> but whoever listens to counsel is wise.
>
> Proverbs 12:15 HCSB

For some bizarre reason, humanity believes itself to be infallible when making decisions. We think that we are the be-all and end-all of wisdom and knowledge. We make plans without seeking wise advice, believing that our own counsel is all that's needed. We think, plan, and execute, sometimes without any outside guidance or wisdom, and often fail because of it. Then we ask ourselves, *"Why didn't it work out?"* Maybe, just maybe, we needed to get suitable sound counsel.

As I mentioned in Week 16, I like to work on and rebuild cars when I can find the time. It's something to take my mind off the pressures and weights of ministry, but it can also be a huge frustration. Sometimes, I optimistically tackle a project, sure I can do it, only to realize that it is beyond my ability, and sadly, I must start over. I could have saved myself time, energy, money, and disappointment if I'd sought wise counsel before throwing caution to the wind and diving in headfirst.

> *"Listen to your elders' advice, not because they are always right, but because they have more experiences of being wrong."*
>
> Unknown

I don't know; maybe it's as simple as I want to be the one who did it. I need to learn to ask more questions and listen to people who are wiser than me. It isn't easy, but if we want to succeed in life, we must ask for help. I mean, why reinvent the wheel? If it works, don't fix it. People have been there and done it, so why not take the time and effort to pick their brains and gain wise counsel. Why be a fool when you don't have to? Being a fool doesn't necessarily mean we aren't smart, but rather that we failed to ask the right questions.

THINK ON THIS... Do you struggle to ask for advice? Does it pain you to admit you don't know everything? Do you pride yourself on trying to go it alone?

WEEK 18
WISE COUNSEL

Day 87

Plans fail when there is no counsel,
but with many advisers they succeed.
Proverbs 15:22 HCSB

As a pastor, I have a key leaders' meeting every week, and we discuss everything in great detail. I would not want to lead without anyone else's input. I'm grateful for the counsel I receive each week from them. There have been times when I've made decisions without their advice and later regretted it. It wasn't that what I'd decided was wrong; it just wasn't the best decision. Sometimes people will run an idea by me after a service, or in the hallway, etc., but I won't decide on my own. I would instead run it by the leadership group first before giving them an answer.

It's so easy to think of something, have a great idea, or a "eureka," moment; however, it doesn't always have the merit we thought it did when presented to a group of advisors. It's incredible what insight and wisdom others come up with. To lead in a bubble is to bring ruin to yourself.

There are times when we've come up with a plan but then decided not to implement it immediately. As we reviewed it week by week, we have found the wisdom to make the project more successful. Taking the extra time and effort allowed everyone to think it through. Not only did the plan take shape, but we also fine-tuned it. With many advisors, there comes creative ideas and the wisdom to make appropriate and necessary adjustments.

> *"No man is so foolish but he may sometimes give another good counsel, and no man is so wise that he may not easily err if he takes no other counsel than his own. He that is taught only by himself has a fool for a master."*
>
> Hunter S. Thompson

My daughter, Bailey, regularly commutes to Nashville to write songs with other talented and gifted writers. What used to be a one-man show has developed into group sessions. While a song written by one can be good or even great, when it is subjected to others, it has the potential to become the best it can be. Why? There is wisdom in the counsel of others who have significant experience and gifting in that particular area. Yes, what you have imagined is excellent, but it can always use a little tweaking by other people who know what they are doing. If you lack wisdom in an area, find those who have experience in it and talk to them. You don't have to go it alone. You know the old saying, *"Two heads are better than one even if one is a cabbage. head."*

THINK ON THIS... Plans are necessary, but wise counsel can improve your plans. Take time to share your dreams with others, listen to their advice, and your plans will certainly gain a greater chance of success.

WEEK 18
WISE COUNSEL

Day 88

Listen to counsel and receive instruction
so that you may be wise later in life.
Proverbs 19:20 HCSB

Have you ever asked yourself these questions after suffering the indignity of a failure or a disappointment? *"If I had only listened? Why didn't I listen? My parents told me many years ago, but I ignored them."* I think everyone could say yes to this at some point in their lives. Hindsight is 20/20, as they say. It's much easier to know the answer after the fact. Experience can be a great teacher, but so can listening. Sometimes we experience negative things later in life because we didn't listen earlier on. The whole point of listening is to give wisdom for the future.

While we may not always want to listen to others, we need to understand that listening isn't necessarily for the present, but also the future. I mean, isn't that what instruction is all about? We learn many things in life, but not all of them can be used today. If we refuse to listen to what is offered today, we might not be able to use it tomorrow. I'm sure you can remember the times when you were doing something, and suddenly, a thought came to you, *"Oh, yeah, I remember that guy telling me about this years ago. I see it now."* We need to remember that God designed the human with two ears and only one mouth, meaning we should do twice as much listening as talking. The reality is usually much different; we like to talk much, much more than listen. I've learned to listen to everyone I talk to, whether young or old.

There is so much to be gained from everyone, even those you wouldn't think have much to offer.

> *"We should get in the habit of continually seeking His counsel on everything, instead of making our own common-sense decisions and then asking Him to bless them."*
>
> Oswald Chambers,
> *My Utmost for His Highest*

The Bible is full of wisdom and knowledge, and anyone who will read it and follow its guidance will have success in life. Young or old, it doesn't matter; the words of God bring great counsel into our lives. Anyone can partake and become instantly wise. Wisdom abounds in the Bible, but it's up to us to read it and glean from it.

> *"If any of you lacks wisdom, let him ask of God, who gives to all liberally and without reproach, and it will be given to him.*
>
> James 1:5

THINK ON THIS... Although I have gained more wisdom and experience as I've aged, I still find the need to listen to others; how about you?

WEEK 18
WISE COUNSEL

Day 89

Counsel in a man's heart is deep water;
but a man of understanding draws it out.

Proverbs 20:5 HCSB

A man of deep understanding will give good advice,
drawing it out from the well within.

Proverbs 20:5 TPT

Not only do we need wise counsel at times, but we will also be required to give it. Have you ever heard the phrase, *"Let me sleep on it and get back to you?"* I've learned that providing the "quick" answer isn't the wisest thing to do. Worse yet, is answering before we hear the whole story. If we think about something long enough, we can usually come up with a good solution. Even better would be to spend time in the Word of God and prayer and let the Holy Spirit give His input to the situation. I can't tell you how many times this has happened to me. Taking a day or two to mull things over can be very beneficial. Proverbs tells us to ponder the paths of our feet and to think things through before acting.

> *"There are two things which a man should scrupulously avoid: giving advice that he would not follow, and asking advice when he is determined to pursue his own opinion."*
>
> Norm MacDonald

> *"A good man produces good out of the good storeroom of his heart. An evil man produces evil out of the evil*

storeroom, for his mouth speaks from the overflow of the heart."

Luke 6:45 HCSB

Our heart is equated to a well full of life-giving water, that when drawn from, can be a fount of great wisdom and counsel, bringing new life to any situation we face. The heart, or the spirit of man, is a vast storeroom that holds whatever we place in there. Out of the heart flows the issues of life or death. When I give counsel, I want to have good things come from my heart, but it all depends on what has been allowed in it. This is why we must spend time meditating on the Word of God and causing it to grow in our hearts, for out of the heart, the mouth speaks. If we want to be people who give good, godly advice, we must keep our hearts free from evil and only allow good things to remain. You have probably heard this old saying, *"Garbage in, garbage out."* If a well is stuffed full of junk, nothing good can come from it. Fill your heart with good things, and that's what will come out.

THINK ON THIS... Take your time when making crucial decisions, and don't be hasty to respond. Learn to 'sleep on it.'

WEEK 18
WISE COUNSEL

Day 90

Oil and incense bring joy to the heart, and the sweetness of a friend is better than self-counsel.

Proverbs 27:9 HCSB

Self-counsel might be the worst counsel we can receive. Is it possible that we believe our own counsel to be the wisest and best? The problem with this is that we are not usually the best judge of our own hearts and character. For example, we often judge other people's behaviour, but only judge our intentions. It's easy enough to think our ways are pure and right all the time. We can believe ourselves to be perfect, but the Lord weighs our motives.

> *"We should not judge people by their peak of excellence; but by the distance they have traveled from the point where they started."*
>
> Henry Ward Beecher

People who only tell you what they think will please you will not be a reliable source of counsel, for they will keep you from seeing the truth. For instance, I have told married couples that they should not go to close friends or family if they need counselling. Some folks have gotten upset with me over this, but I stand by my advice. If you want an unbiased opinion, you probably won't receive it from those closest to you, who are possibly blinded by their great love for you. I'm not saying you should never get advice from them, but the risk of biased opinions is there.

> *"In giving advice, seek to help, not to please your friend."*
>
> Solon

If it's a marriage problem, I suggest talking to someone who has no vested interest in your marriage. Likewise, it's best to receive counsel from people that are not trying to steer you in a particular direction. The best counsel usually comes from people who can look at the situation without prejudice of any kind and will gain nothing from whatever the outcome.

Possibly the worst counsel we can receive is from ourselves. You know what I'm talking about - we can be very negative and hard on ourselves. Sometimes we can't see the good in our lives, or within us. That's when a good friend can be helpful and be a source of encouragement when we need it. A good friend will tell you the truth, even if it hurts a little. If you can find a friend like that, you have found a good thing There are times in every one of our lives when we simply can't see the sun for the clouds covering our hearts and minds. I can be somewhat pessimistic at times, but I have some optimistic friends. They are a breath of fresh air for me when I'm smothering myself with pessimism. Thank God for friends that pour the oil and incense of life on us. We all need them.

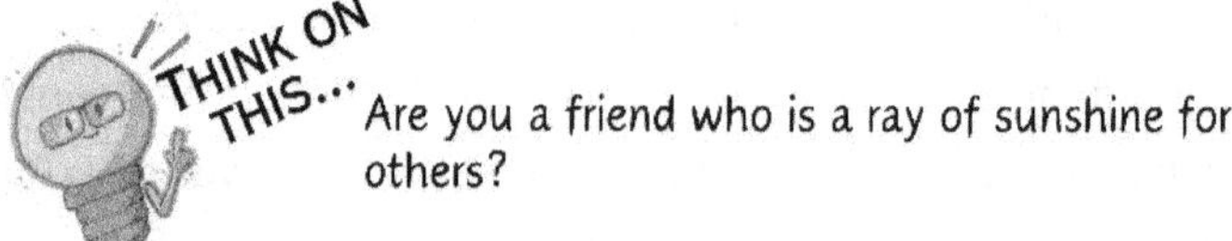

Are you a friend who is a ray of sunshine for others?

WEEK 19 - THE TONGUE

Day 91

The Lord hates six things; in fact, seven are detestable
to Him: arrogant eyes, a lying tongue, hands that shed
innocent blood, a heart that plots wicked schemes,
feet eager to run to evil, a lying witness who gives false
testimony, and one who stirs up trouble among brothers.
My son, keep your father's command,
and don't reject your mother's teaching.

Proverbs 6:16–20 HCSB

The early church leader, James, says that the tongue is evil and cannot be tamed, as it spews forth both sweet and bitter. He also adds, "This ought not be."

Here the writer addresses the lying tongue as one of the seven deadly things God hates. Yes, you read that right, hates! He even calls them detestable! Wow! Detesting is an even stronger emotion than hatred. This clearly shows us just how much God abhors the lying tongue. That is understandable since God is our standard and the very definition of truth. God is incapable of lying, and He has never put himself into a position where He had to. While many people aren't outright liars, some will lie if they think it is necessary to save face or justify themselves. In my many years of pastoring, I've had good Christian people lie right to my face to keep the truth from me. I know why they do it - they want to look good in front of me. However, they don't realize that I'm not their standard or judge. Only God can fill those shoes.

> *"Oh, what a tangled web we weave, when first we practice to deceive."*
>
> Sir Walter Scott

Lying is one of the original sins. When God questioned Cain about his brother's whereabouts, he lied, saying, *"Am I my brother's keeper?"* I'm amazed at the lengths people will go to try to look good in the eyes of others, but I can also understand that we come by it naturally.

Children may learn to lie at an early age to escape discipline or to get their own way. As they grow older, lying becomes a natural part of their living experience. Some folks become such great liars that you would need a lie detector to reveal it. The problem with a lie is that you have to keep remembering it. Who can do that? Eventually, you will get caught in it. If you tell the truth, you don't have to have a good memory.

THINK ON THIS... Telling the truth is still the best policy!

WEEK 19
THE TONGUE

Day 92

There is one who speaks rashly, like a piercing sword;
but the tongue of the wise brings healing.
Proverbs 12:18 HCSB

In the *Merriam Webster's Dictionary*, sarcasm is defined like this:

"1: a sharp and often satirical or ironic utterance designed to cut or give pain.

2a: a mode of satirical wit depending for its effect on bitter, caustic, and often ironic language that is usually directed against an individual."

I grew up in a home where sarcasm was the norm. We learned how to live with it and, unfortunately, became quite proficient at it. However, I soon found out that sarcasm was not the forte for many people and, for good reason - it hurt. For the most part, the sarcasm coming from me was innocent enough, my mode of operation, if you will. I had to learn from the Bible what kind of speech was healthy and what wasn't. The words that we speak are powerful, for both good and bad. Sometimes we talk rashly, without thought, and end up causing pain in the hearts of people. Harsh, cutting words can pierce like a sword, going deep into the spirit of a person. The old saying, *"Sticks and stones may break my bones, but words will never hurt me,"* is totally untrue because words do hurt and cause pain.

> *"Sticks and stones may break our bones, but words will break our hearts."*
>
> Robert Fulghum,
> *All I Really Need to Know I Learned in Kindergarten*

Conversely, the tongue can also be used to bring health and healing. Wise people learn this and seek to use their words to bring grace, mercy, and edification to others. We can make a difference in any situation, no matter how difficult, if we choose our words wisely. Too often, we speak without thinking or allow our emotions to direct our comments, causing more harm than good. I guess this is partly why the book of James encourages us to be *"slow to speak and quick to hear."* As a child, I remember quoting "sticks and stones" when other kids were mocking me while inwardly thinking, that isn't true. The words they spoke did hurt. I said it anyway, perhaps trying my level best to overcome the strength of their taunts, usually, to no avail. When we went home from school, it was often with a heavy or hurting heart. The truth is that our words can either hurt or heal. Let's be wise and speak healing words.

THINK ON THIS... Do your words cut or do they heal? Take the next week and keep track of the words you speak. What will they reveal?

Week 19
The Tongue

Day 93

A wicked person listens to malicious talk;
a liar pays attention to a destructive tongue.
Proverbs 17:4 HCSB

Not only are we taught to watch what we speak, but we are also instructed to be vigilant about who or what we listen to. We are to watch our tongue and the tongues of other people. While it's one thing to control our own words, we are to be extremely careful about listening to the malicious talk coming from others. Those words can be just as dangerous. Our comments are not harmless. They are seeds that contain the fruit of what is spoken. Healthy words contain health; critical words contain malice. Words always contain something, either good or bad. If we like listening to people who speak evil, then we become as wicked as they are. While we may not be guilty of saying the words, the fact that we are listening to them is an indictment just the same.

> *"Wrongdoers eagerly listen to gossip; liars pay close attention to slander."*
>
> Proverbs 17:4 NLT

> *"Evil people relish malicious conversation; the ears of liars itch for dirty gossip."*
>
> Proverbs 17:4 Message

It is not enough to refrain from evil speaking. We are to stop our ears from listening to it too. Our ears are not garbage cans, and yet, that's how we treat them. People allow all kinds of junk in and then wonder why that they struggle later on with people and things. They are bearing the outgrowth of words previously heard. We need to realize that whatever we put in our ears will end up in our hearts, and we will bear the fruit thereof. If we don't stop them from getting in, they will negatively affect our lives. We can't stop the birds from flying around our heads, but we can surely prevent them from landing.

> *"How would your life be different if...You walked away from gossip and verbal defamation? Let today be the day...You speak only the good you know of other people and encourage others to do the same."*
>
> Steve Maraboli

If we find ourselves attracted to malicious talk of any kind, we need to do a self-diagnostic and figure out why. What makes us want to hear bad things about others, like gossip or criticism? Do we secretly love to speak negatively about other people, to criticize family, employers, or leaders? If we do, it's time to reassess our hearts. When other people speak improperly, take a stand against it. If you don't, then those words have the power to affect you.

THINK ON THIS... What kind of friends do you have? Do they serve the Lord and motivate you to do the same? Do they tell you the truth or just what you want to hear? Be honest – are they good for you or not? Choose your friends wisely!

WEEK 19
THE TONGUE

Day 94

The one who guards his mouth and tongue
keeps himself out of trouble.

Proverbs 21:23 HCSB

Have you ever said something that you wished you could take back because it caused you trouble? How about a lie? You once told a lie, and now someone is calling you out on it. What do you do? Do you keep on lying? We have the inherent ability to shoot off our mouths without thinking and thus, cause ourselves all kinds of grief. This only occurs when we forget to put a guard over our mouths. I have a good friend who, in jest, likes to shush his wife when she talks. He says, *"Shhh."* I like that. We would all be better off if we would learn to shush ourselves. I don't know if "shush" is a word or correct English, but it works.

> *"Words are like arrows. Once loose, you cannot call them back."*
>
> George R. R. Martin

This is the problem, isn't it? Once we speak words, they cannot be taken back. Once loosed upon the earth, there is no recovering them. How many times have we thought to ourselves, *"You idiot, why did you have to say that?"* At least that's how I talk to myself. How about this one? Have you ever made a quick promise to someone before you had a chance to really think about what you were promising? You said you would do this or that, not comprehending the price or cost you would have to pay to keep your word.

"In whose eyes a vile person is despised, But he honors those who fear the Lord; He who swears to his own hurt and does not change;"

Psalm 15:4

This refers to someone who has sworn to do something for someone, and even if it hurts or costs, they still do it. This Psalm says this is the kind of person that comes close to the Lord. God prizes people who keep their word, especially if it costs them something. I remember times when friends would promise to do something with me and then bail because they found a better offer. It always hurt me, and I promised myself not to do that to others. I didn't want them to go through what I did. Not only will our loose lips cause difficulty for us, but we can also inadvertently hurt others in the process. It's one thing to utter words without thinking, but quite another to keep them. In this age where words don't mean much, we need to be a people of our word. If we want to keep our lives free from undue predicaments, let's be more cautious about what we speak.

THINK ON THIS... Let's be more purposeful with our words from this time forward. I know our lives will improve as we do.

WEEK 19
THE TONGUE

Day 95

A ruler can be persuaded through patience,
and a gentle tongue can break a bone.

Proverbs 25:15 HCSB

Sometimes we think that to get something done, we need to be forceful about it, but is that really true? According to this Proverb, the best way to influence another is by patience and kindness. When people talk with me and want me to see things their way, I tend to reject them if they are forceful, rude, or controlling. But if they come with humility, a good argument, and a soft tongue, I am more than willing to hear them out. The truth is that when someone speaks to us in a loud and obnoxious manner, we usually respond in kind. If we feel we must use strong words, yell, scream, etc., to get our points across, are they valid? Maybe it isn't much of a point at all. If, on the other hand, we speak gently and patiently, our case is more apt to be heard.

> *"A soft answer turns away wrath, but a harsh word stirs up anger."*
>
> Proverbs 15:1

I've had people confront me about things in a harsh and angry manner. If I react to them gently, they usually calm down and become rational. If I respond in the way they approached me, then the whole situation goes awry. Soft words have the power to change people. Unfortunately, harsh words are usually met with more harsh words.

> *"The tongue has no bones, but is strong enough to break a heart. So be careful with your words."*
>
> Irina Swart

How you talk to people matters. There is a way to speak to people that makes them more susceptible to listen to you. If you want your voice heard, then speak softly and gently. It may seem counterintuitive to do so, but it works. People respond better to soft words.

THINK ON THIS... If you want to be heard, pay attention to how you speak.

WEEK 20 – PRIDE

Day 96

Pride comes before destruction,
and an arrogant spirit before a fall.

Proverbs 16:18 HCSB

The almost all-knowing Google describes pride as *"Having or showing a high or excessively high opinion of oneself or one's importance."* If this is so, then these are the telling signs that a fall is about to occur. For example, let's consider the fall of Satan (Lucifer).

What was Satan's sin that caused his downfall? It was pride, wasn't it? He began to measure himself by his own skewed viewpoint, and the consequences were devastating as he was cast out of God's eternal presence. Lucifer began to think of himself more highly than he ought to have. Was he an important angel? Did he shine? Was he given extraordinary gifts and talents? Was he close to God? Yes, yes, yes, and yes! But he took it too far. He began to equate himself to God. He began to think that he was actually like God. Why shouldn't he be the top dog? The Bible tells us that he said to himself, *"I will ascend, I will be seated up high, I will be like God."* The danger of pride is that it leads to faulty thinking, which in turn leads to arrogance and improper actions.

> *"Humility is not thinking less of yourself, it's thinking of yourself less."*
>
> Rick Warren

The *Merriam Webster Dictionary* describes arrogance as *"an attitude of superiority manifested in an overbearing manner or in presumptuous claims or assumptions."*

Someone exhibiting an arrogant spirit thinks and acts in a superior manner. They falsely assume that they are smarter, wiser, or better than everyone else. They may have foolishly listened to their own press and elevated themselves accordingly. Unfortunately, the end of arrogance is a fall of some kind. What goes up must come down! This is why we must let others praise us and not do it ourselves. It is extremely dangerous to our mental and spiritual health to think we are superior to others.

> *"For I say, through the grace given unto me, to every man that is among you, not to think of himself more highly than he ought to think; but to think soberly..."*
>
> Romans 12:3 KJV

There is a right and proper way to think. It is to have the mindset of humility - having an accurate estimation of oneself - not based on pride or arrogance. If we remain humble about who we are, we can avoid the pitfalls of pride and the spirit of arrogance.

THINK ON THIS... Do you think more highly of yourself than you ought to?

WEEK 20
PRIDE

Day 97

When pride comes, disgrace follows,
but with humility comes wisdom.

Proverbs 11:2 HCSB

Uzziah became king when he was only sixteen years old, and he did what was right in the eyes of the Lord. Through the spiritual guidance of the prophet, Zechariah, he succeeded at everything he put his hand to, and the kingdom flourished.

> *"But when he became strong, he grew arrogant and it led to his own destruction. He acted unfaithfully against the Lord his God by going into the Lord's sanctuary to burn incense on the incense altar."*
>
> 2 Chronicles 26:16 HCSB

Uzziah lost his youthful humility and allowed pride to enter. When his heart was lifted up, he grew arrogant. Why? Maybe Zechariah was no longer able to guide him. Regardless of the cause, arrogance was birthed out of his pride. As a result, he ventured where he did not belong, even as a king. His vanity regarding his own importance motivated him to burn incense on the altar, a task initially ascribed to the priests alone. Pride is self-delusionary. The proud in heart believe they are above the law. Pride thinks along these lines, "*Who are you to tell me what to do? Who are you to put yourself above me? Can't you see how great and important I am?"*

> *"In reality there is, perhaps, no one of our natural passions so hard to subdue as pride."*

Benjamin Franklin

The truth was that Uzziah was indeed great and powerful. He didn't need to add anything to what God had intended for him. The deceitfulness of pride blinds us to the truth of who or what God has made us to be and causes us to chase after what we don't need. We are already who God says we are. We don't need anything more than that.

While he was offering up incense, the priests tried to talk sense into him. Instead of seeing their wisdom, he became enraged. At that very moment, he became afflicted with leprosy and stayed that way until his death. When King Uzziah realized the error of his ways, it was too late. Because of pride, he lost the wisdom he once had as a humble and teachable young man. Uzziah stayed leprous for the rest of his days - not a fitting end for a great king.

THINK ON THIS... Are we content in whatever position we find ourselves? Do we secretly desire a higher place or rank? Let's not be like Uzziah, who became a disgrace because of pride.

WEEK 20
PRIDE

Day 98

Everyone with a proud heart is detestable to the Lord;
be assured, he will not go unpunished.

Proverbs 16:5 HCSB

One of the worst things about pride is that it stops us from listening and receiving advice from other people. The spirit of pride stands tall on its own, wanting and needing nothing from others. As a result, the proud in heart struggle when someone tries to give them a warning or instruction about their lives. I remember talking to a fellow and encouraging him not to do as he intended. I knew it would not end well for him or his family if he went ahead, but I could not get past his pride. In fact, he became visibly upset with me as I tried to pastor him with wise counsel and godly insight. So often, I've witnessed life turn out badly because someone refused to listen to wisdom from people who have been there and done that or can see what they can't. Rest assured, if our pride causes us to shut our hearts and minds to wisdom, we will pay the price. It may not come today but mark my words – It. Will. Come!

Perhaps this is one reason why God hates pride. God, who desires to see His children blessed in every area, would view the proud in heart as detestable. He has provided us with His Word, His people, and the past experiences of life to help us. When we refuse to give heed to good, solid reasoning or advice, what can He do? His hands are tied.

"In general, pride is at the bottom of all great mistakes."

John Ruskin

I wonder how many times we have erred simply because of the pride of our hearts. For whatever reason we don't want to listen. Maybe we thought we knew better, and who were they to offer their advice to us? Perhaps we don't listen because we have tried extremely hard to become an adult. As such, we are no longer children, and fully capable of making our own decisions without input from others. If we want to make good choices, we must do away with this immature thinking. Life is not a contest to figure out who is the smartest or the wisest. We weren't born knowing everything, and we will most certainly die the same way. Usually, what we learn comes because we humbly listen to someone more knowledgeable or wiser than ourselves. When pride is rearing its ugly head, know that if it's not put down, it will hurt us.

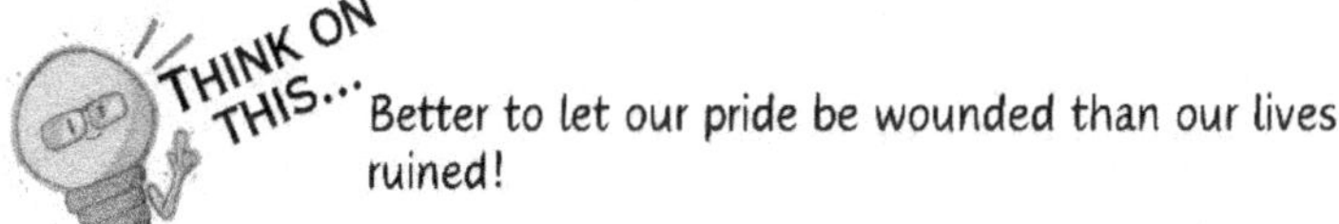

Better to let our pride be wounded than our lives ruined!

WEEK 20
PRIDE

Day 99

A person's pride will humble him,
but a humble spirit will gain honour.

Proverbs 29:23 HCSB

Have you ever felt humiliated? It can happen when we do something foolish or embarrassing in public. It could occur when you are in a group, and everyone is bugging each other in playful jest, but you were irritated when your turn came up. They were joking, but you took it personally.

If you can't take a joke, then you have too much pride. If you find yourself at the butt end of an unintended slight or comment, and it irks you, you have too much pride. If you have looked foolish in front of other people and it really bothered you, guess what - that's pride! If you can give it but can't take it, then you have pride. We have all felt the sting of humiliation at one time or another, and how we feel and deal with it speaks volumes about the level of pride we are carrying. However, if we can shrug it off or laugh at ourselves along with everyone else, pride will not gain a foothold.

"The acceptance of humiliation alone shows the depth and reality of our humility."

Nivard Kinsella

I'm sure we all believe ourselves to be humble, but we will never know for sure until we are faced with humiliation. When we allow ourselves to become angry when we are humiliated, our pride increases, and we become extremely difficult to be around.

We don't take advice, we're always seeking affirmation, we struggle to laugh at ourselves, and get uptight, especially when in a group. The fear of humiliation can cause people to isolate themselves. Rather than learn to laugh at ourselves, or take it all in stride, we eventually stop hanging out with people. Better to isolate and be safe from the possibility of humiliation than to enter the arena of life, or so one can reason.

The truth is, that at one time or another, we all will have to deal with the sting of embarrassment. The question is, will we allow it to humble and mature us, or will we let ourselves become angry and foster the sin of pride?

THINK ON THIS... How do you deal with humiliation? Do you laugh it off or take it personally? Are you better for it, or worse?

WEEK 20
PRIDE

Day 100

The proud and arrogant person, named "Mocker," acts with excessive pride.

Proverbs 21:24 HCSB

The word "excessive," in the original Hebrew, literally means *"an outburst."* This verse is talking about having an outburst motivated by pride. It means to boast about oneself in an arrogant manner, contrary to the truth. Have you ever boasted about yourself, and it wasn't quite the truth? Did you fudge it a little so you could look good in the eyes of someone else? Maybe you weren't outright lying, but it wasn't necessarily the truth, the whole truth, and nothing but the truth, so help me, God. We often attempt to create an image of ourselves that is greater than what we really are.

Suppose we were humiliated when we were young and didn't handle it well. In that case, it's possible that we learned to defend our actions by speaking more highly of ourselves than we should have. We learned to defend our honour by lifting ourselves up with outbursts of pride. It's also possible that we learned to "mock" others because as we put others down, we secretly felt lifted up ourselves.

"Pride must die in you, or nothing of heaven can live in you."

Andrew Murray

When we understand who and what we are in Christ, pride begins to fall away. In our identity as children of God, we are secure in who we are. We won't need to defend our honour or boast of our greatness because we understand our position in Christ. No longer do we need to fight to keep our pride intact or put others down to lift ourselves up. Through grace, God does away with the power of pride when we humble ourselves. When grace is ours, the temptation for pride is destroyed.

THINK ON THIS... The only boast we should offer is about what the Lord has done for us.

WEEK 21 – SATISFACTION

Day 101

Sheol and Abaddon are never satisfied,
and people's eyes are never satisfied.

Proverbs 27:20 HCSB

Just as Death and Destruction are never satisfied,
so human desire is never satisfied.

Proverbs 27:20 NLT

I think The Rolling Stones were on to something when they penned this song about dissatisfaction in life,

> *"I can't get no satisfaction. I can't get no satisfaction. Cause I try and I try, and I try and I try. I can't get no; I can't get no..."*
>
> I Can't Get No Satisfaction
> The Rolling Stones (1965)

Nothing seems to satiate humanity's desire for satisfaction. As we delve into new things, fulfill our deepest desires, and achieve our wildest dreams, we still feel the need to discover something else to bring fulfilment and contentment into our lives. We try new things in the hope that it will finally fulfill our desperate need to feel satisfied, but it doesn't. How many relationships will it take until we are happy? We work on project after project, and still, no happiness. After the honeymoon period is over, the dissatisfaction slowly creeps in, be it in marriage, a new job, a career change, or whatever, it's always the same. How much money does it take before we are content? Satisfaction is difficult to find.

> *"The soul's deepest thirst is for God Himself, who has made us so that we can never be satisfied without Him."*
> F.F. Bruce

The problem is that we cannot be satisfied with dollars and cents, relationships, or careers. Outward things cannot satisfy inward desires because human desire is never mollified. There is a hole in our hearts that our Creator, the Father, left there on purpose. It was a marker designed to remind us that as human beings, we can never be truly happy until that which is missing is found. The "missing desire" in our hearts is God Himself. The longing we have for true satisfaction will only be found when we ask Jesus to come into our lives and take His rightful place on the throne of our hearts. When mankind sinned thousands of years ago, it left a gaping hole, if you will, a separation between God and man. In His infinite wisdom, God set into motion the plan of redemption through the arrival of His Son, Jesus, the Christ. When Jesus was crucified on the cross at Calvary, the penalty for sin was atoned, and the separation between God and His people was dissolved. Now when anyone comes to God, through Jesus,

He will come in and fill that void. Only in God can we find true contentment, peace, fulfillment, and satisfaction.

THINK ON THIS...

Only in Christ can you find absolute satisfaction. Have you allowed Him into your life?

WEEK 21

SATISFACTION

Day 102

> The leech has two daughters: "Give, Give!" Three things are never satisfied; four never say, "Enough!": Sheol; a childless womb; earth, which is never satisfied with water; and fire, which never says, "Enough!"
>
> Proverbs 30:15–16 HCSB

An old saying that I've heard throughout my life is *"Gimme, gimme, my name is Jimmy."* I think it's trying to express that no matter how much you give to Jimmy, he will keep asking for more. When is enough, enough? When do we stop asking for more of whatever it is that we desire? This Proverb tells us four things that will never say, *"Stop, I've had enough!"* They are - hell, the barren woman, the earth that is dried, and the fire that consumes all that it can for as long as it can until there's nothing left to burn.

What lessons do we glean from these passages? What instruction, wisdom, or values can we take from them? For starters, we can look at the leech, who constantly has its hand out crying for someone to give it something. Leeches – what are they? Anyone who has ever swum in one of Saskatchewan's smaller and murkier lakes has likely had a few run-ins with leeches. They are worm-like, dark-coloured creatures that literally "leech" onto the human body and suck their blood. Most leech sightings are accompanied by frenzied screams of horror from the one who has been swimming. Leeches are leeches. They function as they were created to - they leech. They never say, *"Enough, I've had enough blood!"* They always want more.

"There comes a point in every man's life when he has to say, enough is enough."

Lance Armstrong

When is enough, enough? Will we ever get to the place in our lives where we could honestly say, *"Enough, I've had enough. I don't want anymore. I am content and satisfied. I'm happy?"*

I believe the wisdom we need to grasp from this Proverb is don't to be like the big four. Eventually, we need to get to a place in our lives where we can honestly say, *"Enough. I have enough money, friends, prestige, power, and things. I am finally content."*

THINK ON THIS... Have you come to the place where you can honestly say, 'I'm satisfied?'

WEEK 21
SATISFACTION

Day 103

> The one who loves money is never satisfied with money,
> and whoever loves wealth is never satisfied with income.
> This too is futile.
>
> Ecclesiastes 5:10 HCSB

Scrooge McDuck had a humungous money vault that he would jump into and swim around, laughing and giggling with glee. He had so much money that he used it for a swimming pool. His mice even ate it. But as rich as he was, he was always worried about it being stolen. As a result, he became a scrooge. When money causes people to become miserly and fearful, it no longer satisfies. The only time I ever saw Scrooge McDuck happy was when he learned to give his wealth away. Money simply cannot satisfy by its own merit. Far too often, what we pursue eventually loses its lustre, and we end up frustrated and dissatisfied. Why? Because the material things in life can't give us the real and true satisfaction we crave.

The one who loves money cannot be satisfied with it. Money and wealth, by themselves, are merely tools with which we can purchase things. Does this mean money is evil and must be avoided? No, not at all! Money does make the world go around. To be sure, we need money, not only to meet our needs, but also to use for the benefit of others. If I have money and give it away to those in need, will it not make both of us happy? Yes, of course, who doesn't like money? We all do, but we must not chase after wealth for wealth's sake, hoping to receive gratification from it. If we do, we will be woefully disappointed.

> *"Our entire life we chase the wrong things because we think having more money and buying more stuff will make us more happy. But it doesn't. You know why a billionaire has 100 Ferraris? Because 99 weren't enough."*
>
> Oliver Markus Malloy

Have you ever thought or said this to yourself? *"If I only had more money, I could be happy."* I have, and it's not true. Think about it for a second. A person could have a million dollars in the bank and still be unhappy. Another could have fifty bucks to their name and be very happy. Life is funny sometimes. Just when we think we will be satisfied because we bought something or received money, it doesn't happen. It's a deception! It's a lie! Oh, we may enjoy the feeling for a time, but eventually, it fades. Easy come, easy go, as they say. This is why the writer of Ecclesiastes penned, *"This too is futile."* Using money and loving money are two very different things. One will bring satisfaction; the other will not and we must learn the difference.

THINK ON THIS... Money only satisfies if it's used to benefit others.

WEEK 21
SATISFACTION

Day 104

A generous person will be made rich,
and whoever satisfies others will himself be satisfied.
Proverbs 11:25 GW

How can somebody live a satisfying life? Is it possible to live in such a way that we can become really and truly satisfied? Too many people are living lives that will not satisfy them, no matter what they do, where they go, or what they acquire. True satisfaction is elusive! Why? Because it can't be found in money, possessions, or wealth. Money is a deceiving commodity. Just when you think you have enough, you desire more. It's this constant desire that produces dissatisfaction. The more we have, the less it satisfies. This is a huge problem for humanity, but thank God, He has given us the answer to this seemingly unending problem. The answer is to be generous and helpful to others. The following is an educational illustration that can help us overcome the horrible doldrums of life.

> *A fight is going on inside me," said an old man to his son. "It is a terrible fight between two wolves. One wolf is evil. He is anger, envy, sorrow, regret, greed, arrogance, self-pity, guilt, resentment, inferiority, lies, false pride, superiority, and ego. The other wolf is good. He is joy, peace, love, hope, serenity, humility, kindness, benevolence, empathy, generosity, truth, compassion and faith. The same fight is going on inside you. "The son thought about it for a minute and then asked, "Which wolf will win?" The old man replied simply, "The one you feed."*

Wendy Mass,
Jeremy Fink and the Meaning of Life

The Apostle Paul wrote, *"It is more blessed to give than to receive."* People are not rich because they have abundance; they are rich when they are generous to others. Whatever we have an excess of, we are to give away. Only by doing so can we experience a modicum of satisfaction. Hoarding can never yield the fulfilment we are looking for. It's a deception. We think that if we attain much, then we will be happy, but that is a misnomer.

"For it is in giving that we receive."
St. Francis of Assisi

THINK ON THIS... Do you feel like something is missing in your life? If so, be generous to someone else, and satisfaction will be yours.

WEEK 21
SATISFACTION

Day 105

The payoff for meekness and Fear-of-God is plenty and honour and a satisfying life.

Proverbs 22:4 Message

You are my satisfaction, Lord, and all that I need…

Psalm 119:57a TPT

The search is on! Early on, we quickly learn that life doesn't always satisfy us. Life comes with ups and downs, good days, and bad, happy, and sad ones. There is no guarantee of happiness, success, or satisfaction, and yet for all that, humanity continues to pursue these things. Many haven't realized the futility of clamouring after what can never bring true fulfilment. The problem is that as we seek after this "mysterious" sense of satisfaction, it leads us into things better left alone. Too late, people find out that the things they used to gain satisfaction from were basically illusions lacking the substance of truth. People end up abusing drugs or alcohol in the hope of being satisfied, but to no avail. These things have no lasting value or significance. Others pursue the avenue of sexual pleasure, bereft of the knowledge that it only leads to addiction, which, as we all know, can never bring lasting gratification. For some, chasing after all the gold at the end of the proverbial rainbow is their search for happiness. No matter what a person thinks will bring them what they want to feel, none of these things will hit the mark.

Only as we humble ourselves and realize that all our self-efforts, no matter how worthy they may be, will not bring us eternal satisfaction. Jesus alone is the antidote for the spiritual and emotional ills that affect us all. God is the Creator of the human race, and only He knows how to meet our deepest needs and bring fulfillment into our lives.

> *"The only one who can satisfy the human heart is the One who made it."*
>
> Author Unknown

Without Christ in our lives, there is no "real" life. The truth is that the missing ingredient called satisfaction is only found in God. Through His Son Jesus, God alone gives us the way to the life we all seek. I pray that as you read this devotion, that truth becomes a reality to you.

THINK ON THIS... Have you found the real 'elixer' of life? His name is Jesus. As you learn to drink from Him, you will never thirst again.

WEEK 22 – FAITHFULNESS

Day 106

Never let loyalty and faithfulness leave you. Tie them around your neck; write them on the tablet of your heart.

Proverbs 3:3 HCSB

If God says to tie something around your neck, it must be super important. As a youngster, my mom made mittens for us, and she connected them with string. These "idiot" mitts, as we referred to them, were created by the necessity of helping irresponsible children like me not to lose them. How? By tying them together and threading the string through the arms of my jacket, the likelihood of losing them significantly diminished. They were necessary for our immediate survival in our Canadian minus 30 to minus 40 Celsius winters. Did her plan work? Well, not always, but you get the point. Just like those mitts were tied around our necks, we need to keep loyalty and faithfulness close – tied around our neck, if you will.

The writer of Proverbs commands us to tie these godly character traits around our necks in the hope that we never forsake them. In fact, he even tells us to go one step further and write them on our hearts. This dynamic duo of faithfulness and loyalty must be supernaturally fastened to our spirits, which is our inner being. Don't leave home without them.

> *"Where the battle rages, there the loyalty of the soldier is proved."*
>
> Martin Luther

In this day of infidelity and broken promises, these two qualities have become extremely difficult to find. People are quick to jump ship when a better one sails by. A promise given is easily broken without a care or concern. Who is loyal anymore? It seems that people are only as loyal as it benefits them. When the advantage of faithfulness is gone, so are they. I could never understand how some folks with whom I have been in a close relationship for many years can suddenly, and without warning, give it up and walk away. They seem to lack that quality called faithfulness, and the string of loyalty around their neck has been broken and lost. Too many have let go of loyalty when the battle intensified, but faithfulness can only be proven in the tough times. It's in these trying times that our loyalty is tested, and of course, it's the time to stay faithful – faithful to God, our friends, and our families.

THINK ON THIS… Is your loyalty affected in turbulent times or situations? Commit today to tie the strings of loyalty and faithfulness around your heart.

WEEK 22
FAITHFULNESS

Day 107

Lying lips are detestable to the Lord,
but faithful people are His delight.
Proverbs 12:22 HCSB

I'm sure we've all had friends or family promise to do something but fail to live up to it. God loves people who keep their word, for He is the God of faithfulness. In fact, God will never alter the words that have left His mouth. What He says, He will do! It's impossible for God to lie. He keeps His Word at all cost.

The biggest issue we must learn to deal with is our expectations, whether real or unrealistic. If we don't deal properly with expectations, we will go from one disappointment to another. We've all been let down at some point in our lives, but how we handle it is paramount to staying in a healthy frame of mind. I've concluded that if I'm promised something, and it doesn't happen, I need to simply let it go. I cannot afford to spend time getting angry or bitter about what a person did or didn't do. That way I don't have any grudges to carry around. If they don't keep their promises to me, that's on their end, and what's it to me?

"The best way to keep one's word is not to give it."
Napoleon Bonaparte

By dealing with unfulfilled promises in this manner, we can keep our "entitlement" expectations at a manageable level. Many people will overpromise and underdeliver; we cannot avoid this. In fact, we all will fail along these lines at some point in our lives. I can give grace when people don't keep their word to me because I know I've probably done the same thing. However, we should do our very best to keep our promises.

> *"Lord, who can dwell in Your tent? Who can live on Your holy mountain? ...one who keeps his word whatever the cost."*
>
> Psalm 15:1, 4 HCSB

God is pleased when we fulfill our promises, even when it costs us. Too often, the promise is not kept because it interferes with something else in our lives. It is at this point where we must choose between keeping our word or doing what we want. I certainly tried my very best to keep my word to my children when they were young. I knew that if I didn't keep my word to them, how would they be able to take God at His? Are there times when it's impossible to keep a promise? Of course, but if we must, let's make sure to carry it out at another time. Even late is better than never, wouldn't you agree?

THINK ON THIS... When you give your word, do you make sure to carry it out? Are you a promise keeper or a promise breaker?

WEEK 22
FAITHFULNESS

Day 108

A talebearer reveals secrets, but he who is of a faithful spirit conceals a matter.

Proverbs 11:13

Has anyone ever said this to you? *"Can you keep a secret? I'm going to tell you something, but you must agree never to share it with anyone. Can you do that? I won't tell you unless you promise."* And you probably responded this way, *"I promise, I promise. I cross my heart and hope to die if I break this sacred trust."* Well, that's what we did in grade school anyway. But you know what, a couple of days go by and there you go, blabbing it to someone, quickly forgetting your vow of secrecy. What we should say is this, *"You can tell me if you like, but I'm terrible at keeping secrets. In fact, don't tell me at all. I don't want to know."*

Some things are better left unsaid if there is a chance that someone's trust will be violated. Human beings can do many things, but being able to keep a secret isn't usually one of them. I mean, if it's a secret, leave it that way. The minute we tell someone else, it is no longer a secret, is it? Technically speaking, there is no such thing as "keeping a secret." You can't keep what was never yours in the first place. Secrets were made to be kept, well, you know, ... secret.

"To keep your secret is wisdom; but to expect others to keep it is folly."

Samuel Johnson

Faithful people can and do keep secrets. It's why they are considered worthy of trust. I have people in my life with whom I can share my secrets, and they will never break that trust. I remember many years ago when I thought that the Lord had told me who to marry. I told one guy, a good friend whom I trusted, and he never let me down. I did it for two reasons; one, so that I could have someone who would tell me later if I was full of it, and secondly, if it did happen, then I could say that I had unequivocally heard from God. It turned out that I had heard from God, and it sure was nice to have someone to talk to about it. Do you have a person in your life that can be trusted with your most precious secrets? If not, find someone that you can share with. They are invaluable. And maybe, just maybe, you can be a secret keeper too.

THINK ON THIS... Are you faithful to what's been entrusted to you? Can you keep a secret?

WEEK 22
FAITHFULNESS

Day 109

Faithful are the wounds of a friend,
but the kisses of an enemy are deceitful.
Proverbs 27:6

The truth can be hard to bear, especially when it comes from a close friend. Why? I guess because we don't think those close to us will ever hurt us, and we know that sometimes the truth hurts. It's different from the pain associated when evil people do us wrong. Deep down, we already know the friend's words are the truth. This is when a wound from a close friend becomes invaluable if we acknowledge it. A friend who will tell us the truth, the whole truth, and nothing but the truth is a resource we should greatly treasure in our lives. We must be careful, for we don't always see these people for who they are.

Invariably, it's easier to believe the enemy's lies than the truth that comes from a friend. We don't always recognize that our friends are only trying to help us when they speak the truth. They are considered faithful friends because they will be honest with us, even at the risk of damaging the friendship for a while. They are devoted to us even when we aren't to them. Our enemies have no such compulsions. They come to us, not with the truth, but with words that make us feel good – words we want to hear – not what we need to hear. They will even lie to make it seem like they are our best friends, when in reality, they are our enemies. True friends will give us a much-needed truth wake-up call when we need it, but our enemies will seek to win us over with flattery and lies.

> *"Flattery is like chewing gum, enjoy it but don't swallow it."*
>
> Hank Ketcham

One method an enemy will use to gain control over you is through flattery and flowery words. King David's son, Absalom, used this tactic at the city gate to win over the hearts of the men who went in and out. His "kisses" were deceitful. He usurped his father, David, not with violence but with sweetness.

I have had people in the church, especially new ones, seek to win a controlling factor in our lives by speaking what they think we want to hear, using flattery and smooth words. They declared their faithfulness to us, all the while lying both to themselves and us. They only cared about what they could get from us, which was usually a better position in the church or a closer friendship with the leaders. It's incredibly easy to believe what these people say because their words sound so good to our ears. They butter us up with flattery and acknowledgments, telling us how great and awesome we are. They are not trying to honour us or help us but are doing it for their own gain and position. Now, does this mean that everyone who gives us a proverbial kiss, shows honour, or speaks nice words, is our enemy? Not at all, but we must use discernment to recognize the difference.

How can we tell? Well, most of the time, a real friend will speak the hard things to us, the things we don't necessarily want to hear but are beneficial. They really care for us and will say what is good for us, not just what we want to hear. If you have a person like that in your life, count yourself blessed, for you have gained a faithful friend.

THINK ON THIS… What kind of friend are you? Will you speak the truth, or do you seek to win approval with smooth words and flattery?

WEEK 22
FAITHFULNESS

Day 110

Most men will proclaim each his own goodness,
but who can find a faithful man?

Proverbs 20:6

Many people declare themselves loyal, but who can
find someone who is [really] trustworthy?

Proverbs 20:6 GW

Loyalty. Faithfulness. I'm not sure these old-fashioned concepts are understood or considered valuable and important in today's society. It's not uncommon for people to change relationships, friendships, or even churches, in the hope of gaining money, position or status. Like rats on a sinking ship, they will vacate as fast as possible when the relationship no longer benefits them. Even church people, whom you think would be the most loyal, are prone to these behaviours. As of this writing, I have been in the church world for thirty-eight plus years. In that time, I have seen many come and go, people who strongly voiced their sentiments saying, *"We are with you, Pastor, God has called us here."* The ones who speak the loudest are usually the first to leave. Now, I totally understand that people will come and go in churches. That is normal, for the most part. What I don't grasp is when the ones I counted as the closest of friends, left. Over those years, I've had three very close friends that chose to give up our friendship, something I'll never quite understand. Having said that, I still have many close friends in the church that I treasure and am thankful for. Loyalty still exists in the modern era!

"Faithless is he that says farewell when the road darkens."

J.R.R. Tolkien

Everyone will declare themselves loyal and faithful, but are they really? When crunch time comes, will they remain, or will the struggle of relationship drive them away? After all, it's not easy being loyal to one other. All relationships require plenty of love, forgiveness, and grace to be successful. Loyalty is not tested in the days when everything is light, but rather, in the dark, when we are offended or hurt by those closest to us. Loyalty is measured by our response to those whom we call friends when they disappoint or hurt us. Everyone is loyal when life is going our way, but will we still be found faithful when life is hard?

THINK ON THIS...

Each one of us will have our loyalty tested at some point. Will you pass the test?

WEEK 23 – DISCIPLINE

Day 111

Apply yourself to discipline and listen
to words of knowledge.
Proverbs 23:12 HCSB

Discipline – what do you think of when you hear this word? Usually, it is associated with the measures your parents used when you did something wrong. Have you ever gotten a sound spanking? How about the good ole belt? I remember getting the strap in school and let me tell you, it was no fun! It's easy for us to associate the word "discipline" seen in the Bible with the terms I just mentioned, but that would be wrong. This word, "discipline," means to instruct or be warned about. The writer of Proverbs wants the reader to apply instruction in their lives for the purpose of becoming wiser. This is called discipline.

Discipline is for the sole purpose of becoming disciplined. We discipline ourselves to become better.

"Success is nothing more than a few simple disciplines, practiced every day."

Jim Rohn

So, what are we to do? Proverbs says to listen to words of knowledge. As we listen to knowledge, we automatically gain in life. This should be the reasoning behind any form of discipline we have received, no matter how it was meted out. It was to help us become better listeners. In other words, to help us make better choices in the future. All discipline is for this purpose, and he who listens best increases in knowledge and wisdom.

To apply ourselves to discipline means to work on self-discipline. Instead of letting others discipline us, we should learn to do it ourselves. I discipline myself in life by self-learning, self-correcting, and self-changing. If we discipline ourselves, we won't need others to do it for us. I think that's a much better way to live.

THINK ON THIS... Can you think of any areas in your life that could use some discipline?

WEEK 23
DISCIPLINE

Day 112

Discipline is harsh for the one who leaves the path;
the one who hates correction will die.

Proverbs 15:10 HCSB

I like the way the Message Bible says it, *"It's a school of hard knocks for those who leave God's path, a dead-end street for those who hate God's rules."*

All of life is school, no matter what we believe. We either learn or we don't, it's that simple. God has given us commandments and instructions to learn and understand. Those who grasp them will avoid the School of Hard Knocks. I was once enrolled in this school, and it was by this method that I learned about life. It is one way to learn but certainly not the best. Bad experience can be a good teacher, but there is one better. It's listening to do it right in the first place. Why learn the hard way? I don't know, but we seem to excel at it. Some folks never do learn.

> *"We must all suffer one of two things: the pain of discipline or the pain of regret and disappointment."*
>
> Jim Rohn,
> *The Strive*

Listening to correction is the absolute best way to learn, but who likes to be corrected? Almost no one. We all suffer from this malady, don't we? Even if the correction is warranted or good for us, we still hate it.

I remember when I was first saved and gave my life to Jesus. I didn't know what was going to happen or what a believer's life was supposed to look like. I soon learned that when I did what was right, life got better. I realized that I had been in the School of Hard Knocks and still hadn't learned anything. I kept banging my head on the wall. Even though it hurt, I still did it. As I began to gain knowledge of the Bible and apply it to my life, things changed for the better. But I had to admit I was wrong and take Godly instruction and correction. It wasn't always easy, and I had to acknowledge that my pride sometimes interfered with the whole process, and still can today.

THINK ON THIS... Have you ever attended the School of Hard Knocks? Can you think of a time that if you had only listened, things would have gone better? The next time correction comes your way, how will you respond?

WEEK 23
DISCIPLINE

Day 113

Do not despise the Lord's instruction, my son, and do not loathe His discipline; for the Lord disciplines the one He loves, just as a father, the son he delights in.

Proverbs 3:11–12 HCSB

Do you remember when Cain was angry because God hadn't accepted his offering? God, the loving Father, came to correct him and point him in the right direction. He told Cain that if he didn't listen, sin was lying in wait to overcome him. However, Cain rejected his heavenly Father's advice and gave in to the temptation, sadly ending his brother, Abel's life. God tried to save him, but Cain allowed his hatred to override good instruction. Now, his eternal moniker is set for all time as "the first murderer."

> *"The pain of self-discipline will never be as great as the pain of regret."*
>
> Anonymous

We must learn not to hate being disciplined and recognize that it is always for our own good. God is the world's best Father, and he delights in His children, but He also knows that all children need discipline. Some folks may not understand that God never asks us to do what He, Himself, won't do first. He is not a neglectful Father, and as such, will do what is necessary to teach and train His children with discipline.

How does God discipline His children?

1. Through the Word of God
2. Through the conviction of the Holy Spirit

3. Through His people

These are just three of the ways God deals with His people. You need to know that God does not discipline through sickness, disease, and disasters. He does not send tornadoes to punish a city, nor does He put us in the hospital to get our attention, as some foolish souls believe. God is more than capable of teaching us without using extremely distasteful measures. God is a good God and disciplines by instruction and correction. The book of Hebrews tells us that we have listened to our earthly fathers, even though they corrected us for their own profit, whereas God corrects us for our profit. God doesn't correct or discipline out of anger as we are prone to do, but in love, for our benefit.

THINK ON THIS... Never fear the Lord's involvement in your life. He's always working for your advancement.

WEEK 23
DISCIPLINE

Day 114

The one who will not use the rod hates his son, but the one who loves him disciplines him diligently.
Proverbs 13:24 HCSB

I was visiting a family many years ago, and their children were squabbling over something. I thought the father would jump in, but he said this to me instead, *"I usually just let them figure it out for themselves.*" While this sounds good in theory, it doesn't work. Children left to themselves will eventually bring shame to their parents. Children do not train children; that's the parents' responsibility. Too often, this is the norm in a society where fathers are absent, mothers are overloaded, and children are left to themselves. Statistics show that trouble is soon to follow when parents are negligent in child training.

In other instances, parents are hesitant to discipline their children for fear of offending them, perhaps thinking, *"If I discipline them, they will hate me."* While I can understand their inclinations, the truth is usually the opposite. I grew up with a friend who had an older brother who was not disciplined in the least. He was obstinate, disobedient, and rebellious, always in trouble, and difficult to handle. Having learned from their first son, they changed their tactics with their second, my friend. As a result, he was obedient, easy to get along with, and excelled in life. The good news is that eventually, the older brother did settle down to become a good and productive member of society, but not before causing more than a few gray hairs on his parents' heads.

> *"Tolerating bad behaviour is the same as training defiance and rebellion in the heart of your child."*
> Matthew L. Jacobson

If we refuse to discipline, we may believe we are loving the child, but in truth, we are hating them. Real love does what is right for the child. Withholding discipline seems like love but is far from it. If we don't discipline them, then we aren't correctly training them. We warp their understanding of what proper discipline is. If we protect them from all correction, then they will not be able to discipline themselves.

THINK ON THIS... The next time you struggle to discipline your child(ren), remember that it is an act of love.

WEEK 23
DISCIPLINE

Day 115

If you reject discipline, you only harm yourself; but if you listen to correction, you grow in understanding.

Proverbs 15:32 NLT

Too often, we are quick to ignore or disregard that which is good for us, not realizing the harm we are causing. I'm sure that we've all been guilty of this at some point in our lives. I understand why, as we don't like making mistakes and certainly don't like when they are pointed out. After all, our pride is at stake. If we continually reject instruction or correction, we will hurt ourselves. It may not manifest right away, but, trust me, it will. We cannot escape if we reject it.

"No one is as deaf as he who will not listen."

Anonymous Proverb

Why is it that some individuals are always in trouble? Why are the prison systems overloaded? People break the law all the time and wonder why they must pay the piper? We get a speeding ticket and cry foul like the speed limit doesn't apply to us.

When I was about eleven years old, two of my buddies and I decided we needed to have a wiener roast. We planned to steal a package of them from our small-town grocery store. As usual, me, being the brave (or stupid) one, I volunteered. I went in, acting as inconspicuously as an eleven-year-old can, and shoved those weenies into my pants and tried to walk out. The owner grabbed me, and the gig was up. Rats! When my parents found out, I received a well-deserved spanking. When it was all said and done, my mom asked me, "*Why didn't you just ask me for some hot dogs?*" What was I thinking? I don't know. I refused to listen, knowing full well that stealing was wrong, but I tried it anyway. I ignored instruction to my own hurt yet again.

THINK ON THIS...

Ignore instruction at your own peril!

WEEK 24 – TRUST

Day 116

Trust in the Lord with all your heart, and do not rely on your own understanding; think about Him in all your ways, and He will guide you on the right paths.

Proverbs 3:5-6 HCSB

Too often, we plunge into life, making decisions without taking the time to seek the Lord's guidance and end up making mistakes that could've been avoided. I know; where do we draw the line between using our understanding or His? Do we need to ask God about every little thing and seek His advice in every small decision? No, I don't think so, but we can also get to the place where we don't let Him into our daily lives at all. We can err on the side of *"our own understanding,"* if you will, and then regret it when things don't turn out – if only we had placed a little trust in the Lord.

"We need to do what we can do and let God do what we cannot."

Joyce Meyer

I think that our biggest problem when it comes to trusting the Lord for something is we don't want to wait for it. Impatience might be one of the greatest hurdles to genuinely trusting the Lord. We simply want everything right now. We may think to ourselves, *"Well, I could delay this decision while I wait on the Lord. Nah, I'll just do it. What's the big deal anyway?"* For the most part, not a problem; most decisions are not major ones. I mean, do I have to ask God what pair of pants I should wear today, or if I should buy a coffee on the way to work? No, that is silly. After all, God has also given us the ability to choose. However, if it is a major decision, one that could alter our lives either positively or negatively, then we ought to trust in the Lord and let Him give us guidance and direction.

THINK ON THIS... Trust in the Lord with all your heart; the life you save may be your own.

WEEK 24
TRUST

Day 117

Trust in the Lord with all your heart; do not depend on your own understanding. Seek his will in all you do, and he will show you which path to take.

Proverbs 3:5-6 NLT

To trust in our own understanding is to try to use our wisdom, knowledge, and experience to lead and guide our lives. God is telling us not to rely on what we possess but on what He possesses. God has never been stumped! There is no problem He can't solve, no dilemma He can't take care of, and nothing is too difficult for Him to figure out. Have you ever been in a situation where you thought, *"I don't know what to do, and I don't think I'm going to make it through this?"* I have, and as difficult as it is to do at the time, we must trust in the Lord with all our heart. The good news is that we never have to give up because God never does. He has never lost a battle. If we choose to trust in Him, then all of God's resources begin to work for our benefit. God is love, and He always does what is best for the object of His affection.

> *"Faith isn't a feeling, it's a choice to trust God even when the road ahead seems uncertain."*
>
> Dave Willis

God is a good Father who has nothing but the best in store for His children. If we had earthly fathers who did what was best for us, how much more will our Heavenly Father give good things to them that trust Him to lead them in the best possible path?

The struggle that arises is that we may not have had good and reliable role models in the past to trust in. Perhaps you never had a father, or an authority figure you could trust, and they let you down. Maybe you have a problem with trusting anyone, let alone a God you cannot see. You must learn and start to put your whole trust in Him, for if you do, He will not fail you. We can fully trust God because we know that He has our best interests at heart.

THINK ON THIS... Our understanding is limited, but God's isn't. We can only see what is directly ahead, but He sees what is around every corner and curve.

WEEK 24
TRUST

Day 118

Anyone trusting in his riches will fall,
but the righteous will flourish like foliage.

Proverbs 11:28 HCSB

This is most certainly referring to a person who believes that they will be delivered from or kept safe in times of trouble because of their sizeable bank account. The idea here is that if one sets his heart on money, then he unknowingly marginalizes the Lord in his life. We know that anyone who does this will eventually become disappointed as money cannot save them.

Money and riches were never meant to be a source of safety from the troubles of life. Only God has the power to save and deliver us from evil. Money should not and cannot be trusted; it is only a tool and nothing more.

> *"Wealth is the slave of a wise man, the master of a fool."*
>
> Seneca

Money cannot buy you happiness, nor can it purchase a good marriage or family. Riches will not bring peace with God or give you a place in heaven. Salvation cannot be purchased for any amount. Have you ever bought something new, and it brought a measure of happiness? You were happy for a time, but that soon wore off, and it became just another item on your list of things acquired. Riches are deceitful because they promise so much but deliver so little. You can only achieve true prosperity by becoming righteous in God through faith in Christ.

THINK ON THIS...

Expect to flourish as you place your trust in God.

WEEK 24
TRUST

Day 119

The fear of man is a snare, but the one who
trusts in the Lord is protected.

Proverbs 29:25 HCSB

Fear of man is when we struggle to be ourselves in the presence of another person. For some reason being in their vicinity causes us anxiety, fear, and insecurity. Are we afraid to offer an opinion or speak up about something in someone else's presence? It is also evident when we are overly concerned about other people's opinions of us. We second guess every decision we make, wondering what they will think. In fact, this fear can be so crippling that it eventually paralyzes us into doing nothing, hence, a snare.

> *"The greatest fear people live in is the fear of what other people think."*
>
> Sayingimages.com

Now I do not advocate living a life where we never listen to what others say or be insensitive to their feelings, but I encourage you to break free from the fear of man. Stop allowing that fear to paralyze your life! The only fear we should have is a healthy fear of God. Our respect for the Lord will override all other concerns and motivate us to do what is right before God. At that point, what man thinks becomes moot. When we trust in God, meaning we desire to believe and do what He wants us to, it becomes a source of protection from the fear of man. While we must be respectful of others and listen to their wisdom when appropriate, we should, by no means, be scared to live out our lives as we see fit. Only God has that power over us, so why be afraid of people? When you fear the Lord, you won't fear anything else.

THINK ON THIS...

Trust in the Lord and break the power of fear!

WEEK 24
TRUST

Day 120

A greedy person provokes conflict,
but whoever trusts in the Lord will prosper.
Proverbs 28:25 HCSB

According to Roman Catholic theology, the seven most deadly sins are ordered this way: pride, greed, lust, envy, gluttony, wrath, and slothfulness. Number two on the list is greed, which stems from the heart of an insecure person who wants more than what is right, just, and fair. A greedy or covetous person will do almost anything, often resorting to conflict and strife to acquire what they want. The problem with greed is that it is never satisfied, so those people never prosper. True prosperity is more than having everything a person desires. In fact, when we expect more than we ought, it will cultivate a longing for even more - a deadly and insidious cycle, indeed. The more we desire, the worse we become.

> *"Greed is a bottomless pit which exhausts the person in an endless effort to satisfy the need without ever reaching satisfaction."*
>
> Erich Fromm

As we trust in the Lord, He meets the deepest longings of our heart. When we find Him in our lives, all greed starts to evaporate. We no longer have the need to grasp whatever we want because what we once desired no longer satisfies. Thus, greed is eliminated from our lives. God is the only One who can truly give us what will satisfy. He made us for Himself, and He knows what we need and how to meet those needs. He is, after all, our Creator!

THINK ON THIS... The next time you find yourself grasping for more than you should, give your head a good shake and find your contentment in Jesus.

WEEK 25 – SLANDER

Day 121

You must not go about spreading slander
among your people; you must not jeopardize
your neighbor's life; I am Yahweh.

Leviticus 19:16 HCSB

The problem with gossip is that it can quickly and easily turn from seemingly innocent words to slander. *"Did you hear about so and so?"* Blah, blah, blah. Harmless? No, not really, but worse if we slander.

Some other translations describe this word as destructive speech, that is, words that defame someone else's good name. When we slander, we are assassinating another's character. In fact, the Lord says that when we speak badly about someone, we actually put their life in jeopardy. Honestly, I have never thought about slander in such a way, but if God says it, then it must be true.

I can see the truth in this because when we assassinate another person with our words, those who listen may take on the same perception or attitude toward them. We are spreading false witness against our neighbour, thus breaking one of the big ten commandments.

> *"My initial response was to sue her for defamation of character, but I realized that I had no character."*
>
> Charles Barkley

I love Charles's response to slander. He certainly has a wonderful sense of humour, and I think he makes a good point. Don't take what other people say about you too seriously, knowing full well you have probably done the same at one time or another.

Someone may say, *"What if what we are saying is true?"* It doesn't matter if it's true or not - it is still slanderous, and it's still wrong. We are not anyone's judge or jury. Only God has that power and ability, for He hears it all. We, on the other hand, usually only hear one side of any story.

Why do we find it so easy to talk badly about people? I don't know, but I believe we can change that behaviour. When I first became a believer and read the Bible, I came across a verse that I wrote out and taped to the mirror in my bathroom. I read it every time I was in there, eventually memorizing it. To this day, I try to obey, not always successfully, but I keep at it. I would read it in the morning and then feel bad when I blew it, but thank God, His mercies are new every morning. I know I am much better at it now than I was thirty-eight years ago. Here it is:

> *"Let no corrupt word proceed out of your mouth, but what is good for necessary edification, that it may impart grace to the hearers."*

Ephesians 4:29

If we could all become dispensers of grace and kindness to those we talk with, how much better would all our lives be?

THINK ON THIS... Maybe you should put this verse on your mirror and look at it everyday.

WEEK 25
SLANDER

Day 122

Hiding hatred makes you a liar;
slandering others makes you a fool.

Proverbs 10:18 NLT

Before I became a Christian, if I said terrible things about someone else, it often left me with a feeling of superiority - like I was better than they were. In those days, I had no problem slandering anyone I wanted to. But after I was saved, that was no longer an option. The truth is, we may feel good about ourselves when we slander, but in reality, we are playing the fool. To slander another is to walk the low road, but to lift others up is the higher way. Do we have to knock others down to feel good about ourselves? Isn't this what some folks do? For whatever reason, they need to beat others up to find their own self-esteem. It's folly to speak badly about other people.

> *"Slandering people makes you inferior to them. Getting even puts you on their level. Forgiving shows superior character."*
>
> Rick Warren

Perhaps we are tempted to slander another's reputation because they have wronged or hurt us somewhere along the way. Maybe we have a secret desire to get even or obtain vengeance for what they did. If we are in the business of ruining other people's reputations, we will destroy our own. That's the trouble with slander - it affects everyone to some extent. Slander slays the one spoken of, the one spoken to, and the speaker. No one gets away with maligning another.

> *"But now is the time to get rid of anger, rage, malicious behaviour, slander, and dirty language."*
>
> Colossians 3:8 NLT

THINK ON THIS... Perhaps it's time to take inventory of your heart and see if you find any hate in it. That's most likely the motivation behind any slander coming from your lips.

WEEK 25
SLANDER

Day 123

Never slander a worker to the employer,
or the person will curse you, and you will pay for it.
Proverbs 30:10 NLT

We need to look at this topic of slander in a different light. When we talk badly about our co-workers or employers, we are spiritually taking a bite out of them. If we do that, we will eventually be consumed by each other until there is nothing left of the relationship. Instead of gaining friends, we lose them. Instead of becoming someone that can be trusted, the opposite is now true, and we are looked upon with suspicion. That's what happens when we speak evil at the "water cooler." We lose credibility, and no one will take us seriously because we can't be trusted. Slander will hurt our reputation, maybe more than that of the people we slander. Remember, when we point the finger at someone else, there are always three fingers pointing back at us.

> *"Talking badly about someone else while they aren't there to defend themselves, says more about you than the person you are talking about."*
>
> Inspiring Quotes

If we slander our co-workers and they find out, and they will, they are most likely to reciprocate. A vicious cycle begins, and nothing positive will come of it. Have you ever worked in a place where everyone was against each other, trust was nonexistent, and the atmosphere was stifling? Too often, the tensions originated with slander. The danger of this cannot be overstated. I encourage you to take a check-up from the neck up as it pertains to slander. Take a few days and evaluate every word you speak at your workplace. As you do, whatever respect and credibility you have lost will return.

THINK ON THIS... No one gets away with slander; it will always come back to bite you.

Week 25
Slander

Day 124

Wrongdoers eagerly listen to gossip;
liars pay close attention to slander.

Proverbs 17:4 NLT

Look at that, gossip is mentioned in the same breath as slander! It's so easy to gossip. *"Have you heard the latest about so and so? Did you know? I heard that..."* and it goes on. It seems harmless, but is it? God calls those who listen to gossip, wrongdoers. I don't want God calling me that, do you? Look at what this Proverb states next, *"liars pay attention to slander."* I didn't realize slanderers were liars, but I guess they are. If someone listens closely to slander, they are classified as bona fide liars.

> *"People will question all the good things they hear about you but believe all the bad without a second thought."*
>
> Unknown

This is the crux of it. People are quicker to believe the bad than the good. That's what makes slander so insidious. Good news doesn't sell quite as quickly as bad. If there was no gossip to report, nothing would be said at all. There is nothing like the possibility of wrong that has the power to whet our slanderous souls. If gossip has the power to hold our attention, what does slander do? If we love to hear the latest buzz, then, no doubt, slander will most certainly command our attention.

Well, I, for one, do not want to come under the influence of gossip or slander. If I willingly listen to it, then I am a partaker of it, for the one who pays close attention to slander is also guilty of it. Better to hold out our hands and say, *"Don't tell me! I don't want to know. I think well of those people, and I'm not planning to change that."* Maybe we need to do what I do sometimes when my wife wants to tell me something I don't want to hear. I stick my fingers in my ears and walk away yelling, *"Dah dah dah dah daahhh!"* If I can't hear her, then I won't know it. That sounds like good advice to me.

THINK ON THIS... Next time someone starts to talk badly about another person, stick your fingers in your ears and run away. I think they'll get the point, don't you?

WEEK 25
SLANDER

Day 125

I will not tolerate people who slander their neighbors.
I will not endure conceit and pride.

Psalm 101:5 NLT

God has a big problem with slanderers because He understands the real reason why people do it. A slanderer's stance is one of superiority - the position of the heart that exalts itself. God calls it conceit and pride. Pride caused Lucifer to fall from grace. His sin was to *"think of himself higher than he ought to,"* which led to his downfall. A third of the angels were booted out along with him. For whatever reason, they listened to Lucifer – not the most brilliant move!

> *"What is slander? A verdict of "guilty" pronounced in the absence of the accused, with closed doors, without defence or appeal, by an interested and prejudiced judge."*
>
> Philibert Joseph Rouxo

Slander reveals the pride and conceit hidden in a person's heart. There is no humility in defamation. It is one of the devil's favourite weapons - very similar to accusation. Both are cruel and sadistic. If we have nothing good to say, then we should say nothing at all. That's what I heard from grown-ups when I was a kid, and it is still good advice today.

THINK ON THIS... Speak good things about your neighbours. If we slander them, we shouldn't be surprised if they slander us. Remember – we reap what we sow!

WEEK 26 – HOPE

Day 126

The hope of the righteous is joy, but the
expectation of the wicked comes to nothing.

Proverbs 10:28 HCSB

Hope, what a powerful and life-giving force! Why? Because hope literally means *"confident expectation."* In other words, it is the anticipation that good things will happen in our lives. Life becomes a sad and dreary existence without it, but with the power of hope, all things become possible.

In this context, the writer is saying that the righteous (saved, right with God, believers) have a hope that produces great joy in their lives. The opposite is true of those who aren't righteous. People who have a declining hope or, worse, no hope at all, have no expectations of good in their lives.

Why does hope bring joy to the believer? Because God is the source of their hope, and with Him, anything is possible. God is a good God, and He wants good things for His children. He hears their prayers and gives them the desires of their hearts.

> *"Hope itself is like a star — not to be seen in the sunshine of prosperity, and only to be discovered in the night of adversity."*
>
> Charles Haddon Spurgeon

When God is with you, hope becomes more than a dream, a wish, or a fantasy. He gives you hope - real hope that has a firm foundation. It is more than simple thoughts or words; it is a tangible force. God is the God of hope! We can put our trust in Him because He will not let us down; therefore, our hope will produce joy and happiness. We know that He is working to bring our hopes and dreams into reality.

> *"Faith is the substance of things hoped for."*
>
> Hebrews 11:1

Faith in God brings with it an assurance that what we confidently expect will soon come to pass. He gives His children faith that produces the outflow of hope, which, in turn, brings great joy. Every child of God can expect good from His hand. How can that not produce joy? God has the infinite ability to make our hopes a reality, because nothing is too difficult for Him.

THINK ON THIS... Do you have a confident expectation in God? What are you trusting Him for?

Week 26
Hope

Day 127

Delayed hope makes the heart sick,
but fulfilled desire is a tree of life.
Proverbs 13:12 HCSB

Were you ever promised something that you really wanted? Suddenly, hope sprang eternal, and anticipation began to grow in earnest. If the promise was broken or delayed, what happened on the inside of you? Your heart was affected, wasn't it? Great joy and expectation were now replaced with dejection and dismay. Hope gives us something to look forward to, an expectation of things to come. It has the power to motivate us and empower our lives to move forward. We must be careful because delayed hope and broken promises can produce discouragement and even depression. When that happens, it's easy to lose sight of the good things in life, despairing of all that is good. It's easy to stay focused on what didn't happen. We can fixate on that instead of looking for a better future. Let's face it, we will be disappointed in life, but we don't have to let it control our outlook or emotional state.

"We must accept finite disappointment, but never lose infinite hope."

Martin Luther King Jr.

Although we will have our hopes dashed at some point, we must continue to believe. Things can look bleak, but they will eventually turn around if we continue to hope. Life is full of ups and downs, but we must never let the downs crush our hope for good things in our lives. I have learned that all things are subject to change - nothing stays the same forever. Like an old friend of mine used to say, *"The bus comes by here every fifteen minutes. If you missed it, don't worry, it will come by again."* It's the same with life. We may not see what we want at this very moment, but it will change.

THINK ON THIS... What you hope for may be delayed, but don't give up, for your breakthrough is right around the corner!

Week 26
Hope

Day 128

Don't let your heart envy sinners; instead,
always fear the Lord. For then you will have a future,
and your hope will never fade.

Proverbs 23:17–18 HCSB

Envy - it desires what others have. The problem with it is that it produces hopelessness. Envy steals hope. When we look at what others have, we usually view it from the point of *"Have not and never will."* I wish I had what they have, but it probably won't ever happen for me. Desiring what others have is a dangerous game. It's not good to crave what other people have, nor put our hope in copying who they are. Our trust must be in the Lord. He has a plan for us, and it is good. Do you believe that?

> *"Stop coveting what others have and start asking God for what He knows is best for you."*
>
> Andy Stanley

"Thou shalt not covet..." is one of the big ten that God gave humanity for their benefit. He knows that longing for what others have can cause people to forget about trusting Him. The sin isn't so much about wanting something as it is about desiring it apart from God's will in your life. In God, we have a future; without Him, not so much. Hope doesn't always work to our advantage in and of ourselves, but with God, it burns bright. We only have limited human ability to work with. In contrast, God's ability for us is unfathomable in scope and sphere, without limitations or

confines. We can have endless hope because where God is, hope abounds.

THINK ON THIS... Trust God with your future, for life without hope is no life at all!

WEEK 26
HOPE

Day 129

My child, eat honey, for it is good, and the honeycomb is sweet to the taste. In the same way, wisdom is sweet to your soul. If you find it, you will have a bright future, and your hopes will not be cut short.

Proverbs 24:13–14 NLT

Do you like honey? I do, and I don't know of too many who don't. I eat it almost every day on my toast with peanut butter - another of God's greatest gifts. Honey is sweet, tasty, and good for you. The writer likens wisdom to the traits of honey. Without it, life can become full of bitter consequences instead of sweet rewards, for it helps us make right decisions, that in turn produce good results. A lack of wisdom causes us to make wrong decisions, resulting in less satisfactory outcomes.

"The only true wisdom is knowing that you know nothing."

Socrates

If we continually make bad choices our hope will start to diminish. Unless we gain some wisdom, we may eventually lose all hope. Sometimes, what we hope for is nothing more than a pipedream because we lack what it takes to bring that desire to pass. Hope is good to have when life has thrown you a curveball, but it still won't straighten things out unless you acquire wisdom. Without the wisdom to know who to trust or what to do, hope can be fruitless. Thank God that He has given us all we need to see our hope come to fruition. Trust in Him and read His Word, it contains all we need to see our hopes fulfilled.

THINK ON THIS... Are you trusting God and His wisdom for your life?

WEEK 26
HOPE

Day 130

> The wicked is overthrown through his wrongdoing and calamity, but the [consistently] righteous has hope and confidence and a refuge [with God] even in death.
>
> Proverbs 14:32 AMP

This proverb contrasts what the wicked have versus the righteous at death. One has hope; the other does not. Only the consistently righteous have any hope of eternal life after death. As the wicked draw close to their final breath here on earth, they will not experience this because they don't have that sense of being right with God. When a person has made peace with God by accepting His Son Jesus, that He sent to save them from their sin, they then have this hope for life after death.

I vividly remember a time when I broke one of the ten commandments. At that moment, I thought, *"I have really done it now. I'm on my way to hell if I die."* I instinctively knew that if I was to die at that moment, I was in no shape to stand before God. Any confidence I might have had melted away in that one sin I had committed.

At some point or another, everyone must deal with the idea of dying and what it holds in store for us. While many hold differing views on what happens when they die, we know that only those who are made righteous in God's sight will end up in heaven for eternity.

Is your sense of right standing with God overthrown by your wrongdoing? Can you honestly say that you are righteous before God? I had that same sense that if I had died, I wouldn't be able to enter heaven as a righteous man, but the moment I accepted Jesus into my life, that all changed. When Jesus came into my life, I was transformed from unrighteous to righteous in the blink of an eye. I still remember it as if it happened yesterday, and what a great day it was!

> *"No matter who or what we are, God restores us to right standing with Himself only by means of the death of Christ."*
>
> Oswald Chambers

If you have not asked Jesus to come into your life, today could be that day. It will be the best decision you ever make, and you will be given the confidence of being right with God and be assured of everlasting life.

THINK ON THIS... Right standing with Christ will erase the fear of death.

ABOUT THE AUTHOR

Brent boldly proclaims that anyone who calls on the name of the Lord will be rescued, recovered, and restored – just like he was over thirty-eight years ago when he came to know Jesus and was instantly set free from addiction to drugs and alcohol. Shortly after accepting the Lord, Brent came to Faith Alive. He attended Bible College there, was raised up in ministry there, and has never left. Over the years, he has served in nearly every area of the church, and in 2005 was appointed Senior Pastor. He has developed a deep love for the church, desiring to see it be a fireplace that continually houses the presence of the Lord.

The best way to describe Brent's preaching style is bold and passionate, with a good dose of humour thrown in. His teaching will challenge, encourage, and provoke you to lay aside your own agenda, eliminate the options, and follow hard after God.

As a pastor, Brent's heart yearns to see healthy churches filled with people willing to give their lives to advance the Kingdom of God, both here in Canada, and around the world. Brent longs to see revival and healing sweep from shore to shore in Canada.

Brent pastors Faith Alive along with his wife, Barb. Besides pastoring, they enjoy spending time with their grandchildren, and their little dog, Buddy.

Other books by Brent Rudoski are available on Amazon, or by calling 306-652-2230.

In *Jesus Was Not a Rebel*, you will learn about:

- How you can overcome and walk in the power of God like Jesus did.
- The root cause of rebellion.
- Whether or not Jesus was a rebel.
- Whether rebellion in the church is hindering the Kingdom of God.
- How to break free from the power of rebellion.
- How to negate the effects of rebellion.

The contents of this book can revolutionize your walk with the Lord.

YOU can experience God's compassion that sets you free to move forward with a productive, overflowing life!

Chapters include:

- Mercy – the pathway to blessing
- Failure – it's NOT final
- Attracting God's mercy
- How to handle life's unfairness
- Treating others better than they deserve
- How far should we go in showing mercy?
- Stuff Happens

Faith Alive Family Church, located in Saskatoon, Canada, has a global mandate to see God Rescue, Recover, and Restore people in every area of life. Everyone deserves to experience the Power and Presence of God, and Jesus is worthy to receive all honour and glory!

Faith Alive is a Jesus centred church where our worship is free and without apology. As our voices unite, our hearts are transformed. The preaching is without compromise, and we believe that God is ready, willing, and able to meet you right where you're at.

To learn more about Faith Alive, visit us at www.fafc.ca

CONNECT WITH US

facebook.com/FaithAliveFamilyChurch

YouTube

youtube.com/wwwFAFCca

Mailing Address:
Site 600 Comp 211 RR6
Saskatoon SK S7K 3J9

Location:
304276 Township Rd 372 (Agra Rd)
Saskatoon SK

email: info@fafc.ca

www.ingramcontent.com/pod-product-compliance
Lightning Source LLC
LaVergne TN
LVHW050534160826
845677LV00011B/2025

9781988316321